Bomb on the Red Markers

Pat Cunningham

COUNTRYSIDE BOOKS
NEWBURY BERKSHIRE

First published 2010

COUNTRYSIDE BOOKS
3 Catherine Road
Newbury, Berkshire

To view our complete range of books,
please visit us at
www.countrysidebooks.co.uk

ISBN 978 1 84674 198 2

'Is that a Lancaster? – or a Spitfire?' Wies White, 2010

Designed by Peter Davies, Nautilus Design
Produced through MRM Associates Ltd., Reading
Printed by Information Press, Oxford

Contents

Introduction

Although I joined the RAF six years after most wartime aircrew had left the skies, several officially-designated operational campaigns brought me into at least a peripheral kinship with them. Certainly, aircrews were integral to the 20,000 hours I was to fly during my forty years in Service and Civil aviation. However, while my lodestone was Flight, theirs was to serve Britain in the most telling way.

And that way had been amply prepared for them, with boys' books extolling the exploits of the aerial aces of the 'war to end all wars' and the newspapers untiringly reporting the prowess of aviation's record breakers. Accordingly, as yet another four years of Flanders' mud and blood loomed, it was little wonder that so many felt drawn to the RAF.

By the second year of the war these volunteers were joined by those who had seen what enemy bombers had done to Britain and whose motives included a wish for revenge, although martial ardour was rarely divorced from the enduring romance of Flight, even though the prosaic demand this makes of all its devotees is that they keep their feet on the ground and their heads out of the clouds. Such varied motives, as might be expected, drew an equally disparate cross-section of the youth of both Great Britain and her Empire. There were, of course, commonalities among the volunteers, not least medical fitness and a facility for assimilating technical knowledge. These aside, they came from all walks of life and from every social class.

For class, of course, was very much alive in the forties, and was certainly reflected in the two-tiered structure of aircrew; some commissioned, some non-commissioned. This essentially social distinction even dictated the award of decorations, with crosses for officers (commissioned and warrant, see Glossary) but lower precedence medals for airmen aircrew; a distinction persisting until 1993!

The fact is, though, that such anomalies meant little to the crews. After all, while flying, and while mixing informally on the ground, first names were the order of the day, few having difficulty in 'playing the game' and addressing the commissioned officer as 'Sir' in front of senior officers. As for decorations, most crews remember being far more concerned with surviving than with such fripperies.

For all aspirants the road to qualifying as aircrew was lengthy. Nor did the British weather help a process where continuity was so important, many being sent to train in the clear skies and uncluttered landscapes of South Africa, Rhodesia, Canada, and the United States. For all trainees, though, the final stage was when the various newly-qualified specialisations were melded into operational crews, the vast majority being destined for Bomber Command, although the other commands, Coastal, Ferry – to become Transport in 1943 – and even Fighter, took their share.

Volunteers though they had to be, once having joined an operational squadron, crews were required to fly a first tour of, in the main, thirty sorties, or 'ops'. Those who accomplished this would then be rested – screened – for a nominal six months before being recalled. Except that for many the screening meant flying on as an instructor, an occupation arguably as hazardous as active operations.

On the other hand, former crew members commonly speak of operations forging a bond 'closer than kin', so that rather than risk starting a second tour with untried strangers, many waived their right to rest and flew on. Just the same, of 125,000 Bomber Command aircrew, only 7,000 embarked upon a second tour. To volunteer for a third tour was rare; to complete one, even rarer. Even so, 62% of crews became casualties.

Understandably, faced with such an attrition rate, an inescapable problem among operational crews was that of coping with fear. Many hold that anyone claiming to have felt no fear has simply allowed the kindly years to blank out the memory. But some do maintain that they never felt afraid. For the majority, though, handling fear was something to be worked out by the individual.

One bulwark against everyday harm was the utter faith put in those whose combined efforts got the crews into the air. But it is a concomitant of aviation that due appreciation can never be given to non-flying personnel, the regrettable truth being that, genuine though expressions of solidarity are, the focus is invariably upon the fliers, and far too often, specifically upon the pilots. There was always the trusty fallback, 'It won't happen to me'. But empty beds and vacant places in the dining hall spoke for the reality.

Then there was the moral aspect of aerial bombing. Nobody who had dropped on the training ranges could doubt that a good proportion of the bombs had to fall wide of the rail junction, blast furnace, or oil refinery; just as in London, Liverpool and Coventry, many had to fall on homes. On women. And on children.

One doubter was reassured when his crew argued, 'They started it, the humane thing is to finish it as quickly as possible.' For most, though, the saving grace may well have been that their minds were already over-extended, for having survived the myriad outbound perils and bombed the target, thoughts turned only to the hazards of the homeward flight.

Another factor which militated against fretting about anything beyond the mechanics of the task, was lack of flying experience. Many crew members, screened after full tours, had logged fewer than 500 hours in the air.

Of prime importance, of course, was their youth. Indeed, many completed a tour of operations before their twentieth birthdays!

Yet at any Aircrew Association meeting today even age fades into insignificance. As do high-domed pates, stooped backs, thick-lensed spectacles and walking sticks. Those attending do not inhabit their youth, for modern-day concerns predominate, only the occasional touch of jargon reflecting the experiences shared in that long-gone era: kites, ack-ack, undercart, skipper, dicey, flak, George, stooging about, ropey and, of course, Raff, the latter anathema to the generation that followed on.

Age has, of course, taken its toll, but as in their pre-operational briefings when their world was young, so their indomitable spirit bubbles through.

The story of The Few has been told often enough. These are the stories of just a few of the many, recorded as a tribute to the tellers. But as a tribute too, to the 125,000 who trained alongside them, flew and fought alongside them and, in so many cases, fell alongside them.

The Hazards to Operational Aircrew

That 55,573 aircrew from RAF Bomber Command alone were killed during the Second World War is accepted with awe. Yet the true wonder is that losses were not far higher, especially given that 8,305 of these casualties resulted, not from enemy action, but from accidents.

To those on the ground, the death-dealing bombers seemed omnipotent, yet the aircrews knew how insubstantial they really were. The bomb load was the obvious hazard, but there was petrol too, as well as combustible oxygen, oil, and hydraulic fluid. And there was the ever-present risk of collision, and over the target, of bombs released from higher-flying aircraft.

Once the raiders were on their way, the night sky, immense as it might seem, offered little enough protection. All very well to switch off the navigation lights and to maintain radio silence. Yet even those electronic aids which the crews were permitted to use, not least mapping radars, were too often compromised as the enemy learnt to home in on their pulses.

Then again, each aircraft would be belching out spurts of fire from its exhausts. And as long as the bomber stream remained over enemy-occupied territory, flak bursts and searchlights would attract even those fighters initially sent astray by disinformation. Finally, over the target, the flames themselves threw the raiders into silhouette.

Heavily-laden bombers were also much slower and less manoeuvrable than their fighter opponents and even prior to committing themselves to the run-in had little hope of evading attack once a fighter had made visual contact. All crews were trained in the diving-rolling-climbing 'corkscrew' tactic, but this was poor protection, particularly against fighters firing hard-hitting 30 mm calibre ammunition as opposed to the relatively puny 7.7 mm (0.303 inch) variety used by the British.

The German fighters (see Enemy Machines, page 181) were backed by the ground defences, the searchlights, the sound detectors and increasingly, the radars, and always the anti-aircraft artillery or flak (for details, see Enemy Defences, page 184). In the early days a flak commander might well lose interest in a bomber that had dropped its load and instead turn to the next, still-laden machine, but an ever swelling number of radar predictors allowed multiple targets to be engaged. As for trying to evade, well, which way do you go, when any turn might meet with the next burst?

But the fliers faced natural hazards too. Not least in pitting their relative inexperience against temperate zone weather! Nor could the 'Met' men help all that much, robbed as they were of observations from the Continent. And that was without the gremlins, past masters at causing oil to leak and engines to stop and, therefore, well capable of changing winds and lowering clouds. For bad-weather aids were scarce, even should circumstances permit breaking radio silence, leaving the gremlins to batten onto that perennial hazard to aviation, the lack of an altimeter capable of telling a cloud-bound crew their height above the ground! And especially above the hills that rose only minutes' flying time beyond their mist-prone, sea-level bases in Lincolnshire and Yorkshire. True, radio-altimeters that would do this existed, but they were reserved for such specialised units as the meteorological flights.

Hazards in plenty, then. And each of them, to a body of men well conversant with arithmetic, a constant reminder of just how heavily the odds were stacked against them ever finishing their operational tours.

Pat Cunningham, DFM, RAF 1951–1973

Acknowledgements

To the traced copyright holders authorising the use of their photographs: Richard Haigh, manager, intellectual properties, Rolls-Royce; Nicola Hunt, intellectual property rights copyright unit, MOD; archives staff, Imperial War Museum; Judy Nokes, licensing adviser, HMSO (Crown Copyright/MOD); archives staff, Royal Air Force Museum; craving the indulgence of those for whom all contact attempts have failed.

To Julian Temple and John Lattimore of Brooklands Museum for their Wellington expertise; to Clive Teale, aviator and grammarian, for technical advice; and the photographic staff at ASDA, Spondon, for their cheerful and unstinting assistance.

Despite such inestimable help, any errors remaining, and all opinions expressed, are my own.

Pat Cunningham DFM

Return times to targets, including tactical routings, based upon Lancaster log-book averages

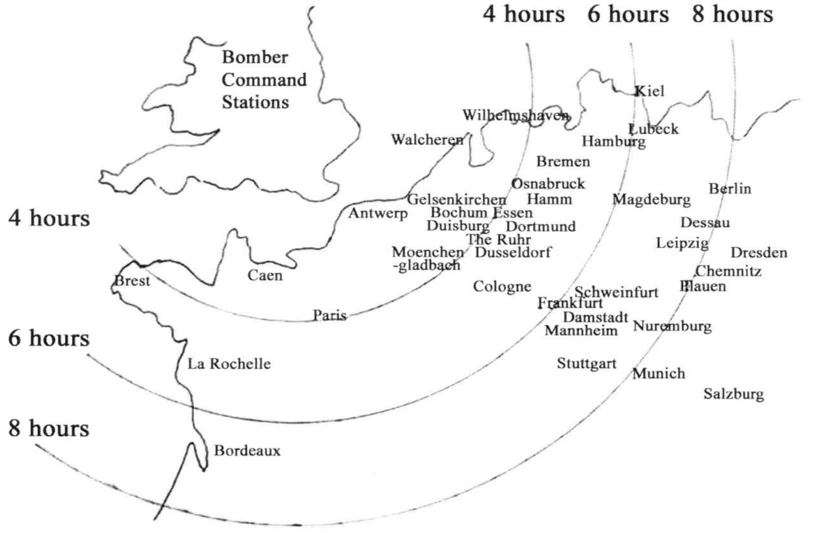

1

Corkscrew, Starboard...Go!

Warrant Officer Dennis (Sandy) Slack
Bomb aimer

In 1937, after leaving school at fourteen, I began my training as a motor engineer with Westfield Transport in Mansfield. Even as I qualified, however, I was being seduced by posters urging, 'Change your overalls for a flying suit!' Not surprising then that when war seemed inevitable I decided to volunteer to fly with the RAF. In fact, five of us applied together, of whom one failed flying training and two were killed on ops.

But that lay in the future when, in August 1941, the selection centre at Birmingham assessed me as 'Suitable PNB' – pilot, navigator, or bomb aimer – and I became an Aircraftman Class Two (AC2) prospective pilot.

After kitting-out, my first real posting was to Cambridge, to No. 2 Initial Training Wing (ITW), where we began to study, among other things, the morse code, navigation, theory of flight and air force law, each subject being taught in a different college. They worked us hard but I thoroughly enjoyed myself, emerging as one of the thirty of our original fifty to reach the required standard.

We survivors then moved on to No. 22 Elementary and Reserve Flying Training School, the wartime guise of Marshall's of Cambridge. This was a grading school where aspirant pilots were assessed during a maximum of fifteen hours' flying instruction on Tiger Moth biplane trainers. These I found a delight to fly, though the open cockpit and the propeller blast made me grateful for our gauntlet gloves and Sidcot flying suits.

I felt that I was making good progress but many more had already fallen by the way as I approached eight hours. I quailed, therefore, when the flight commander, Flight Lieutenant Lund, announced brusquely, 'You're flying with me today.' Once I was at the controls, however, my confidence returned; more so after pulling off two very respectable touchdowns. After the second he bawled, 'I have control,' and scything the tailskid around, powered us back across the airfield, merely skimming the grass. Touching down, and spinning the aircraft about again, this time into the wind, he clambered out of the front seat. 'Do one circuit, then come in and land.' He finished securing his discarded straps. 'Now, off with you.'

And that was how I came to experience that most wonderful – yet most awe-inspiring – feeling of being in control of one's own destiny in the medium of the sky! Additionally, I had passed grading school, my log book recording eight hours and twenty minutes in the air!

A fortnight later I reported to No. 1 Aircrew Despatch Centre at Heaton Park, Manchester, where trainee aircrew destined for the Empire Air Training Scheme received their postings. I found myself among a batch destined for Canada, embarking on the Polish liner MS *Batory* at Gourock, on the Clyde, bound for Halifax, Nova Scotia. The voyage took six days, followed by a lengthy train journey, first to No. 31 Personnel Depot at Moncton, New Brunswick, then on to our flying training school at Caron, near Moose Jaw, Saskatchewan.

After the grass field at Cambridge, Caron's tarmac runways initially made us wonder. However, they proved to be no problem, for the Canadian-built Tiger Moths had tailwheels rather than the skids of the home-grown variety. They also had canopies which made them warmer in winter and could be slid open in summer, allowing us to fly in shirtsleeves. Indeed, that pretty well sums up our concern for the weather, which afforded us a continuity of flying training unheard of in Britain.

I quickly settled to the task once more, delighting in every flight. Not that I steered altogether clear of trouble. On one busy afternoon, approaching to land, I balked an instructor carrying out a practice emergency landing and found myself at a desk, writing out 200 times, 'I must obey the rules of the air'.

In the main, though, things went well. That is, until I had completed some forty hours and they pulled a syllabus-wide snap exam. I was rated a gratifying 'above average' in flying but, despite my mechanical background, I had gone blank during the armament paper, dropping my total mark to 59%. Only the required mark was 60%! And neither leeway nor quarter was given.

At the disposal centre at Royal Canadian Air Force (RCAF) Station Trenton I was told that I could re-train as a bomb aimer, the board president pointing out that as the bomb aimer acted as second pilot my training to date would prove useful. And so, bitterly disappointed though I was, I agreed to change roles, beginning my new career at RCAF Fingal, just across the river from Detroit, in the United States.

Here, we flew in Canadian-built Avro Ansons, with cabin heaters and hydraulically operated, retractable undercarriages. For our advanced training, we moved to Anciette Lorette (now Quebec City airport) where we flew British-built Ansons: 46 turns of the handle to get the wheels up, 46 more to get them down again. Nor was there a heater!

Wearing the provisional 'BA' brevet, 1943.

I did not blank on this course! But only when we finished did someone begin to wonder what brevet this new aircrew category was to be awarded. Initially, a local supplier produced a pilot's double wing centred with 'BA', for bomb aimer, which was so striking that I wore one for a photograph. In the end, though, it was decided that we would wear the observer's 'O' half-wing: it would be some time before the 'B' brevet came in. On the other hand there was no problem with sewing on our three stripes!

Even so, my stripes may well have proved more temporary than they did. 'What about a commission?' the commanding officer smiled at my final interview. What possessed me I have never been able to recall! Possibly some obscure blanking again. For I heard myself saying, 'I believe, sir, that a commission should be earned before being awarded.'

What I remember very clearly is his taken-aback expression. 'Oh,' he said, 'I'd recommended you for one, but as you've clearly given it some thought, so be it.' He then made a crossing-out stroke on my file, congratulated me on completing the course, and wished me luck. And confirmed-senior-NCO 'Sandy' Slack, not a little bemused, about-turned and marched smartly from the office.

January 1943, and everyone was shivering in the moist, Mansfield brand of winter; so different from the Canadian dry cold which seemed much easier to bear. Just the same, merely being back in the family circle was enough to warm me. And things were to get even warmer, for at an otherwise uneventful party I met the most stunning girl!

Betty, her name was, and having spent the whole time in her company, I asked if I might walk her home. Smilingly, she acquiesced, possibly realising that this lay across on the far side of Mansfield. Just the same, before we parted I got her to consent to another meeting the next night.

That tryst, too, went well. Just the same, I only walked her halfway home that night; after all, new love is new love, but a six-mile walk ... Fortunately for me, Betty must have thought I had potential, for she overlooked – but in sixty-six years has never forgotten! – my less-than-courteousness and we continued to see each other for the rest of my suddenly all-too-short leave.

Fortunately, my next posting was to what is now East Midlands Airport and was then RAF Castle Donington, a Wellington Operational Training Unit (OTU).

The task of the OTU was to sort groups of five newly-trained fliers into crews, then teach them to operate the twin-engined Wellington bomber as a step on the road to flying heavies.

My five-man crew comprised: Sergeant Thomas Edwards, pilot; Sergeant Freddie Fields, navigator; Sergeant Dennis (Sandy) Slack, bomb aimer; Sergeant Ernie Whitfield, wireless operator/air gunner; and Sergeant George Chapman, rear gunner.

We settled quickly, and soon became an entity in which each man knew that the others were utterly dependable. This dependability, however, did not extend to the unit's time-expired Wellington Mk1Cs. We were not unduly surprised, therefore, to get airborne on a solo detail and have an engine splutter, cough, then lose power. We made it around the circuit but sank so low that watchers lost us beneath the trees. It was a nerve-straining few minutes but Tom managed to scrape in, to be met by the CO's car, the flight commander's bicycle, the crash tender and the ambulance.

FRANÇAIS!

Le Gouvernement de la Grande Bretagne vient de signer un accord avec le Général de Gaulle, ainsi qu'en témoignent les documents suivants :–

1. Lettre de M. Winston Churchill
2. Texte de l'accord
3. Lettre du Général de Gaulle

Loading propaganda leaflets.

A leaflet dropped in Occupied France.

Advised of the problem, the flight commander tried a start himself. And having got only backfires, 'Right, the lot of you,' he snapped, 'into "G" for George, and get off again.' The philosophy being, get back on your horse before you lose your nerve!

We flew on, and eventually progressed to embarking upon a 'Bullseye', an exercise simulating an operational sortie. The routing was via the Isle of Anglesey, then the Isle of Man – where I was to drop a practice bomb! – to a turning point in Scotland, and back to base.

All went well until we were midway between Anglesey and the Isle of Man when the starboard engine lost oil pressure, leaving Tom no option but to stop it. Freddie gave us a course to the nearest airfield, RAF Valley, back on Anglesey, while Ernie busied himself at his wireless. He had hardly tapped out the first SOS, however, when the set gave up the ghost.

Arriving at Anglesey, and deciding against firing flares into the night and waiting for permission to land – an unhealthy proposition on one, still-windmilling engine! – we turned in on the approach. As we got lower we experienced rather more turbulence than the conditions seemed to warrant, only to realise that we were nose to tail with a Beaufighter landing without lights!

Doing a communal gulp we pressed on, set down in his wake, and were given accommodation for the night. Only to be awoken some hours later as an Anson crew blundered in – thoughtless buggers! – tired and bleary-eyed. And moaning at having fruitlessly searched the Irish Sea for an aircraft which had transmitted an incomplete SOS and was believed to have ditched ... Red faces! Thinking it hadn't gone out we hadn't bothered to report our truncated distress signal!

Back at Donington we duly ended the OTU course on the night of 23 May 1943 by flying a 'Nickel', or propaganda leaflet raid. Four trainee crews were dispatched to Lille, in Belgium, each aircraft operating independently. Freddie did a splendid job of navigating us to Lille, handing over to me so close to the run-in heading that I had little to do beyond giving Ernie the go-ahead to shovel out the leaflets. Tom then turned us about, and we throbbed our way home.

It was our first op! And an easy one, so we began debriefing in a state of euphoria. Until we discovered that only three of our four trainee crews had returned. It was in a sombre mood, therefore, that we left debriefing, the five deaths having taught us that there was no such thing as an easy op.

Having hoped to be assigned to Lancasters we were a bit miffed to get Halifaxes. For a start, they couldn't climb as high as the Lancaster. But on arrival at the Halifax Heavy Conversion Unit at RAF Marston Moor, near York, we were addressed by the already celebrated Leonard Cheshire.

'I know how you feel,' he told us, 'but having flown all three heavies I regard the Halifax as the finest of the lot. Believe me, it'll always look after you.'

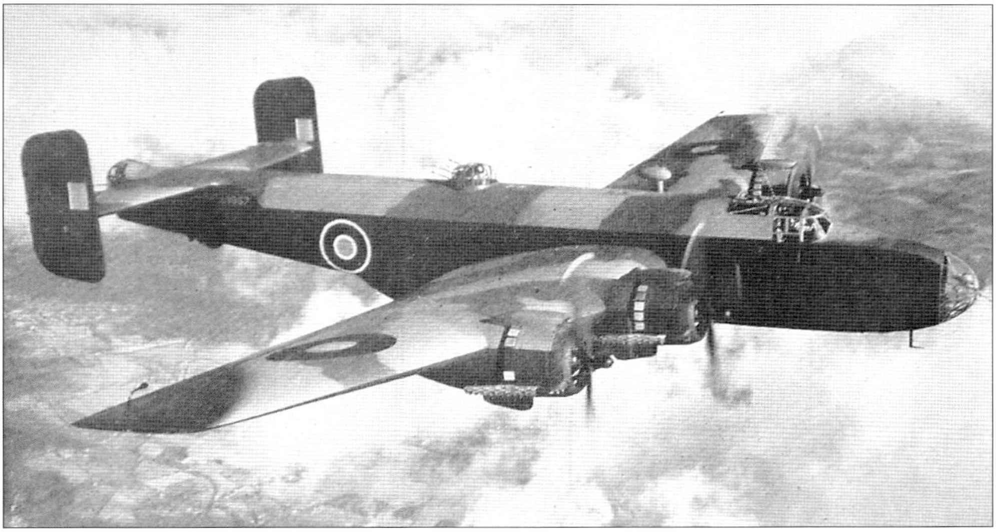

A Handley Page Halifax.

We were not totally convinced, even so we soon accepted our lot. Just as we accepted our two new crew mates: a flight engineer, Sergeant Dick Goddard, and a mid-upper gunner, Sergeant – but what name to give? The first promptly broke his ankle, after which we rarely flew with the same one twice!

In late June 1943 we were posted to No. 158 Squadron, at RAF Lisset, south of Bridlington. Re-enthused by being allocated a Hercules-engined Halifax Mk.3, LV907, newly delivered from the factory, we completed a week's acclimatisation flying, after which we were finally judged fit for operations.

Our machine's squadron letter was 'F' for Freddie, but as usage allowed us to customise what followed the 'F' we decided upon 'F' for – *Friday the Thirteenth*! Besides reflecting its delivery date, we deliberately set out to defy convention, plastering the fuselage with every bad luck symbol we could bring to mind; we even had a ladder painted over the entry door! And it paid off, for 'F'-Freddie was to complete 128 operational sorties and earn a whole crop of awards for the crews who flew her. To this day she is commemorated in composite form at the Yorkshire Air Museum at Elvington.

We flew our first heavy-bomber op on 1 August 1943. For the first time we experienced the rise of tension as we saw our names on the battle order. Then there was the sense of restriction when the station was sealed against private outside communications. Briefing followed when the length of red tape leading to the target seemed never ending.

The composite 'F' – Friday the Thirteenth *at Elvington Air Museum, 2010.*

On it went, ever eastwards, right across France, straight over the Alps, to finally finish at Turin, and specifically at the Fiat works! We were told about the markers to be used over the target, given details of the route, and the weather. Then other specialists detailed bomb and fuel loads, and signals procedures…

After which we were clambering aboard and engines were running and our groundcrews were grinning and raising oily thumbs.

Finally, we were running down the runway, engines snarling at maximum power. Full bomb load and tanks filled to the gills with highly inflammable petrol made this arguably the most critical phase of the flight. And yet, for my part certainly, with tension turning to ease; this, after all, was what I had trained for!

As it turned out, the Turin raid proved a heartening introduction to long-range operational flying. The trouble-free route, the almost unbelievable spectacle of the snow-capped Alps – for all our 18,000 feet, seemingly only feet below – plus the excitement of seeing flak for the first time; and back at debriefing, coolly assessing it as 'just light'. Even so, not all the aircraft returned.

Hamburg was our next target, with the bomber force employing a new aid, codenamed Window, consisting of strips of aluminium foil cut to some correlation with the wavelength of the enemy's radars and designed to confuse their fighter-controllers. Indeed, we learnt later that the enemy had believed themselves to be facing the biggest bomber fleet yet!

Although our tour started off in a rush we did not appear on the battle order every day. But on 9 August 1943 our number came up again, sending us to Essen, after which we understood why the lads called the Ruhr, 'Happy Valley'.

A little later we set off for Mannheim but had only just entered Germany when, disconcertingly, all four engines started running rough. As chance had it, we were not that far from our secondary target so we slid aside from our direct routing home and were able to use our bombs rather than merely jettison them. After that, with only negligible flak to see us on our way, we puttered and spluttered our way back to base and, after a four-and-a-half-hour flight, deposited the engine problem into the laps of our temporarily puzzled groundcrew.

There was never to be a routine about ops, but there were commonalities. We'd get airborne, climb on course, change gear on the supercharger at about 12,000 feet – to restore engine power in the more rarefied air – and carry on to as high as 19,000 feet. In order to avoid areas of heavy flak we'd be deliberately routed over a coastal area judged unsuitable for siting any meaningful number of anti-aircraft guns.

Just light flak ...

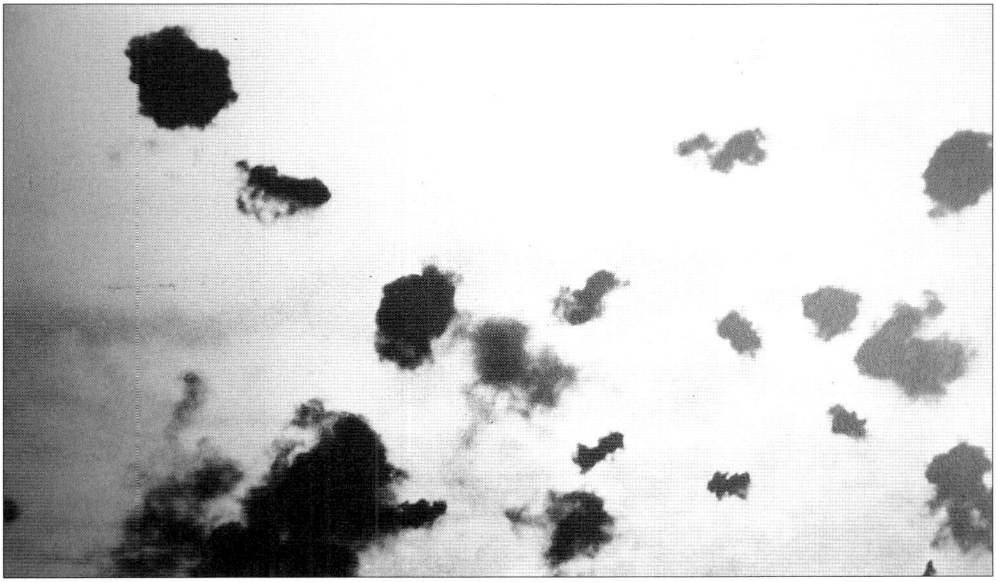

Flak aside, however, things would become increasingly fraught as over 600 unlit heavy bombers funnelled towards the same, relatively tiny, target, each aircraft being navigated independently and no two performing alike, the whole stream to run in and bomb in under twenty minutes!

Not that I had overmuch time to dwell on the outside world. 'Bomb doors open.' The bombs were armed by operating twenty paired switches, or rendered safe, if need be, by reversing the switches. With these set, Freddie's best wind, and the airspeed off my repeater – 140 mph – would be fed into the bombsight.

I would identify the target, then concentrate on the sword-shaped indicator – cast by a light – calling for corrections to the aircraft's heading until the target appeared to flow down its blade, then mouthing fine adjustments, 'Left, left, steady... steady.' And when target and 'cross-guard' coincided I would press the button.

As each bomb fell away, so two pins would release. The airflow would then spin vanes on its nose and tail, one initiating a time delay, the other arming the bomb to explode on impact after that delay.

Mark Fourteen bombsight: when target and 'cross-guard' coincided, I would press the button.

'Bombs gone!' The aircraft would surge upwards. And in lieu of a stopwatch I would begin counting. 'One red motor car, two red motor cars, three red...' and so on up to 'Twelve red motor cars'.

However, just before 'twelve', a very powerful photo flare would illuminate at 2,000 feet. This was arranged to go off just before our bombs exploded, so providing a 'before' picture which could be compared with the next day's photo recce which would supply the 'after' shot. Of equal significance, our photo would also reveal how close to the aiming point I had been!

I talked of the target itself 'flowing down the blade', but for the most part we would not be tracking – or dropping on – the actual target but on a pyrotechnic indicator. The target-marking Mosquitoes would drop a spot-marker flare. When satisfied that this was accurate the raid controller would have Pathfinder Force aircraft supplement the spot marker with red or green target indicators. He would then direct the bomber force to, 'Drop on the red markers', or, if these had strayed, 'Drop just north of the red markers.'

This appointment of a raid controller was itself a sophistication made necessary by the tendency for successive crews to drop earlier and earlier, anxious as they were to get rid of their bombs and turn for home. Exhibiting the exact-same tendency I would be conscious of my red cars getting faster, and then faster, until numbers ten to twelve would race by, unashamedly vying with one another in a sprint finish.

Many a near-norm, however, was cast aside at briefing on 17 August 1943. So that, when the target area was seen to be a small headland jutting out into the Baltic Sea, a puzzled silence replaced the normal groan. Smiling quizzically, the group captain scanned our faces.

'Yes, chaps, a new one. In fact, I don't even know what they've got down there. But this I can tell you: if you don't get it tonight, then you'll be back there tomorrow night. And the night after that, and so on, until you do.'

More surprises followed. There would be 597 aircraft in five waves, and someone called a master bomber, a sort of airborne master of ceremonies, we gathered. But the bombing height was to be just five thousand feet! And this on a moonlit night!

The group captain held up a restraining hand. 'A Mosquito force,' he assured us, 'will overfly the target, then head south for Berlin. This should draw off the fighters.' The 'should' produced a wry response, but in fact the diversion worked well. We duly bombed, the first four waves turning away virtually unscathed. As the fifth ran in, however, the re-deployed fighters appeared, and forty-one bombers failed to return.

Later, when I learnt that the target, Peenemünde, was the development site for not only the V1 and V2 reprisal weapons but also for jet- and rocket-powered fighters, it was gratifying to reflect that our photo-flash had shown my aiming point to be spot on!

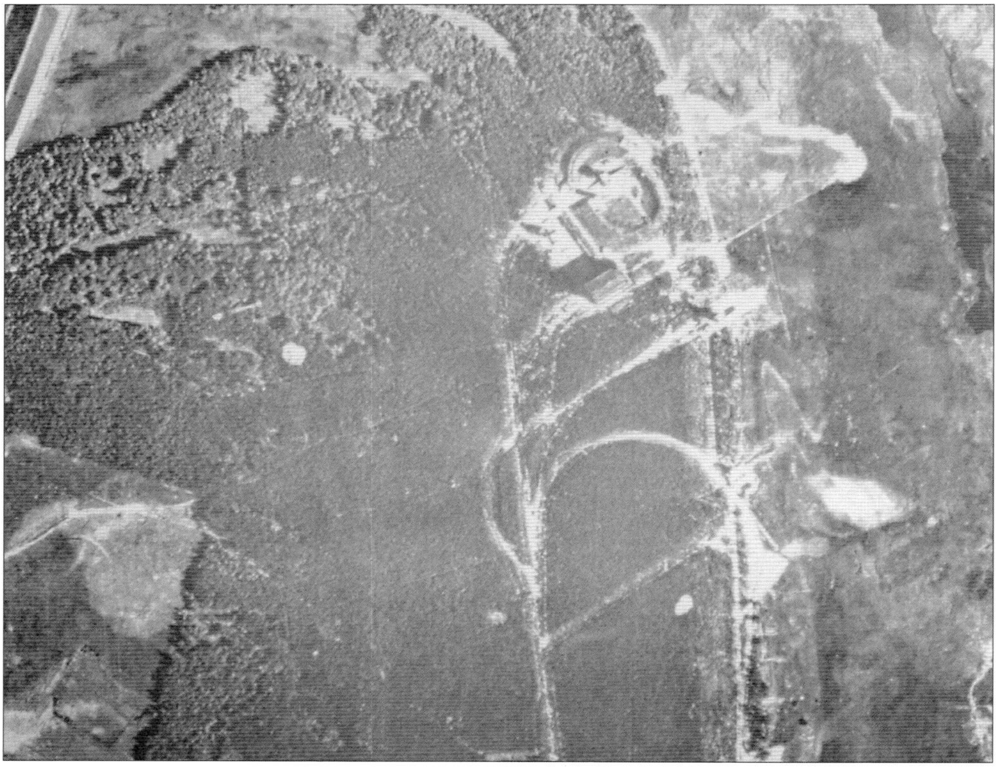

23 June 1943, Peenemünde V2 Rocket site revealed.

Saturday, 22 August 1943. On landing from the pre-op air test we lingered, seeing the fuel bowser approaching. A squint at the driver's clipboard, and we grimaced. This was to be a long one. We trooped into briefing, into an atmosphere heavy with tension and cigarette smoke, and heard just three words: 'Ops are cancelled.' We then joined in the unfettered cheering that drowned the permission to stand down.

23 August 1943. The next day. Prime summer weather. With our groundcrew prepping 'E'-Edward rather than 'F'-Freddie. But an aircraft change was not unusual. What was unusual was the timbre of the howl as the curtain came back. Berlin! Our first visit. And a rare enough target then. Although some were to identify this very day as ushering in the 'Battle of Berlin'.

'The flak defences,' the navigation leader announced, 'are thickest to the west of the city. To keep you clear, therefore, markers will be dropped even further west, beyond range of the guns. As you approach, you'll see reds to your left, greens to your right.

Continue heading south, keeping between them.' His pointer travelled downwards, well to the south of the city, stopping where the red track-tape reversed direction to lead sharply upwards. 'At this point, gentlemen, turn north-east, bombing on that heading.'

'Bloody tight turn, that,' Tom muttered in an uncomfortable sotto voce. But nobody else said anything audible.

The city's opposition was formidable, but in the early minutes George's advisory from the rear turret was quietly controlled, 'Plane going down to starboard, Skipper.' The next casualty report, just moments later, came from the mid-upper. Then as more and more reports filled the intercom, Tom called a halt. 'Note 'em, lads, but keep a sharp lookout for fighters.'

The routing markers floated by as we dutifully continued south. Then came the turn! Tom made it all right, but only by excessive banking. At which point Freddie handed the navigation to me. With the bomb doors open, I threw my switches. Then, flat on my tummy, concentrated on the aiming point.

George spoke swiftly, not wishing to balk my commentary. 'It's that turn, Skipper, the fighters are swarming.' His mic clicked off.

'Steady,' I mouthed, 'steady ... Left, lef... '

Two streaks of light broke my concentration, peripherally demanding attention and only feet away. Christ – *tracer*! A fighter!

'Corkscrew, starboard... go!' I yelled. Instantly Tom banked, and shoved. A moment later, though, bullets began rapping at the bulkhead behind me. Then fragments were flying everywhere, the sounds-off including an ugly crackling.

'Sorry, lads,' Tom's voice was terse. 'We'll have to bale out.'

I craned up, to see Freddie busy unshipping the escape hatch beneath his seat. He gave a hurried thumbs-up, then disappeared, Dick Goddard, the flight engineer, followed suit.

Getting to my knees I saw the mid-upper reach the hatch. I realised too that Ernie Whitfield was still stuffing leaflets down the chute! Then, as more bullets rattled in, the mid-upper was nowhere to be seen, while Ernie was a bloodied heap.

Scrambling upright, I seized Tom's chest parachute, placed it next to him, then clipped on my own. Tom had no time to look around, merely gritting, 'Sandy, get out.'

I sized up the situation. Beyond him, the port wing was a fiery mass. By lingering I could only hamper his escape. *His escape*! A fiction. I knew it even then. But I had no option. Indeed, even as night and the air-rush embraced me, so the port wing folded upwards, sending 'E'-Edward into an ever steepening spiral. Just one of the fifty-one bombers lost that night, including five from No. 158 Squadron.

An age after that I rose to my feet, gingerly at first, but then with growing confidence, and began to take stock. In fact, as training clicked in, the required course of action came to me ready-made: walk west, towards France, and find a Resistance escape line. I pushed my parachute deep into some bushes. I would walk by night, rest up by day.

In the event, I walked for three nights, not turning to my escape and survival kit until the second night. I discovered various bits and pieces, even 2,000 French francs, and two compasses. But best of all, Horlicks tablets. There was also, damn its hide! a tube of condensed milk.

When dawn caught me the only cover I could find was a corn stook. Having crawled inside, I decided to try the condensed milk before getting my head down, only to come to some time later with a raging thirst. That double-damned condensed milk!

Emerging with great care, I satisfied my thirst in a ditch, then returned with equal care. Only not carefully enough, evidently, for a short while later there was a shout of, '*Heraus! Heraus*!' and the barrel of a gun told me that my time as an evader was over.

After a night in a police cell I was placed in the care of two soldiers, a corporal and a private, for a rail and road journey which culminated in my being handed over to the Luftwaffe at the Dulag Luft Interrogation Centre, Oberursel, near Frankfurt.

Dulag Luft, the main Luftwaffe Interrogation Centre at Oberursel, north of Frankfurt.

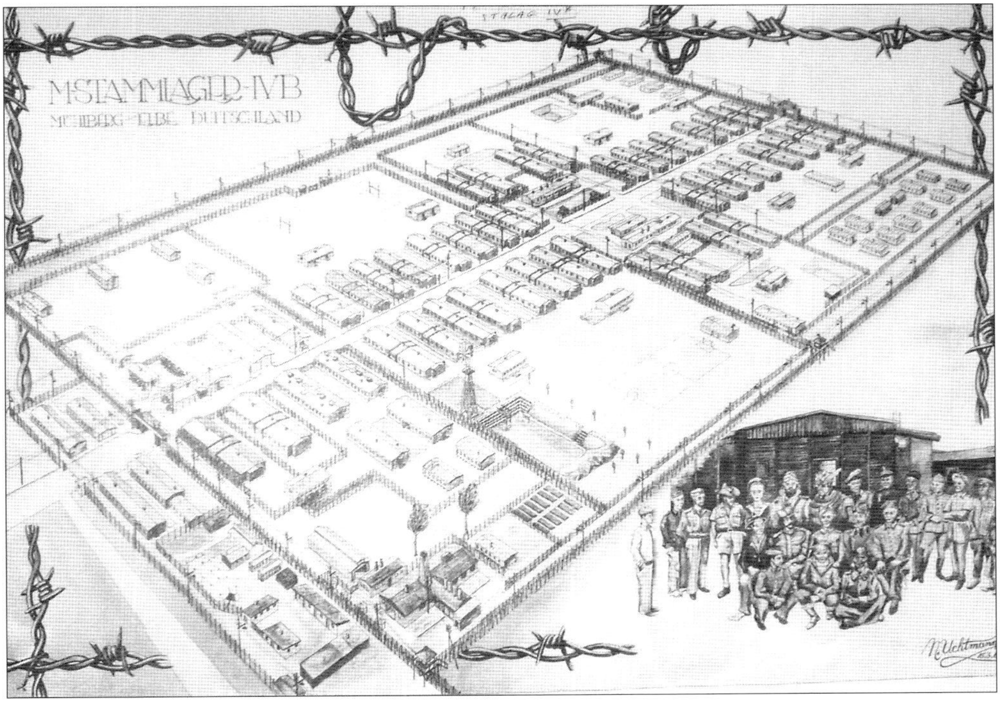

Stalag 4B, Muhlberg, 1943.

Here I was unceremoniously bundled into a tiny cell – two paces one way, three the other – and left alone. In fact, it was eight days before the door opened again. Then an officer entered, carrying a file ostentatiously proclaiming, *No. 158 Squadron*. Being long past apprehensive, I found this laughable. However, when he opened jovially with, 'Squadron aircraft letters NP, yes? We say, NP, no petrol,' I merely shook my head.

He then proffered paper and pen. 'If you fill in this Red Cross form we can notify your people that you are safe.' I obediently scratched away before, assimilating my nonsensical responses, he snatched back both pen and paper and turned on his heel. An hour later I was released into the main camp.

Among a crowd of aircrew I was overjoyed to recognise both Freddie and Dick. Having allocated me a bed they took me to the meticulously laid out dining room to feed me a meal. Only, in my naivety, I thought this was to be the future!

It was a notion that had long been dispelled when, a few days later, about 300 of us were marched through the gates of Stalag 4B, at Muhlberg, some ninety miles south of Berlin.

Stalag 4B was a Wehrmacht camp intended for army prisoners but as the stalag lufts designed for RAF prisoners were full, we were told, we were to remain here until other arrangements could be made. In the interim we were accommodated in a wired-off enclosure containing four large huts; a POW camp, in effect, within a POW camp.

Each hut was fitted with double-tiered bunks and accommodated 200 men. There were windows, but with paper in place of glass, while the bedding comprised straw-stuffed mattresses laid on wooden bed boards. There was a latrine in each hut for night-time use, and a separate toilet block containing forty unscreened seats in the compound. Then, between each hut, there was a concrete washroom with four taps which, at best, merely dribbled cold water.

On arrival we were stripped naked while our clothing was fumigated, after which our hair was sheared. Next, we were photographed and I became POW No. 222643 of Hut 36B, Stalag 4B.

Lights-out came at ten; as did the bed bugs! Next morning, following a complaint, the huts were fumigated, after which we swept up the bed bugs by the thousand: all that personal cleansing, only to deliver us into infested huts!

Camp routine required us to assemble in rows five deep at eight in the morning and six in the evening. As for meals, mid-day dinner comprised a cupful of soup and two boiled potatoes; tea, a small loaf of black bread to be carved between five, with a miniscule pat of butter substitute and ersatz jam. And that was it!

Shortly after our arrival the camp received a further 20,000 British POWs from the Italian and Western Desert campaigns. At the same time it was decided not to move the RAF inmates, a decision which gave us the freedom of the whole camp. As aircrew were regarded as high escape risks, however, we were not allowed to join outside working parties. Indeed, the guards were not too sure how to treat us. In the general way, though, they were quite reasonable, particularly as the war progressed and the potentially more fanatical, younger troops began to be replaced by older dugouts, or men too badly wounded for further front-line service.

Just the same, there was an incident when a German sergeant, having discovered prisoners raiding a coal store, fired blindly through the window, his random venom killing a young warrant officer who only that day had received notification of a DFC.

Not long afterwards there was another killing, when a POW was shot as he ducked under an inner wire to retrieve a ball. They had to call out the guard to quieten us but although we made formal representations I never heard of any action being taken.

We lost another POW when a Luftwaffe pilot decided to beat up the aircrew compound. He made several passes, each one more flamboyant than the rest. But interest turned to horror when he overcooked it and his wingtip took the head off a luckless spectator.

In the main we were not interfered with. On one occasion, though, a sizeable team of

SS were coached in to search all the RAF men. Each of us in turn had to come to a desk and have his belongings vetted, then rubber stamped. Except that one babbling POW objecting at the desk became two, then four, then ten. Until the rubber stamps were appropriated and used to mark everything in sight. At which the SS gave up, boarded the coach and drove off, leaving us jubilant and our guards – who had been patently terrified of them – intensely relieved.

Not long after that the Germans agreed to put up a large wooden hut for use as a school, and subsequently allowed an even larger one to be used as a theatre.

The school was soon offering a vast number of subjects. But the theatre, named the Empire matched it in popularity, seating 600 – front rows reserved for Germans! The shows put on were as ambitious as they were well received: the play entitled *The Women* featured twenty-six POWs in luscious drag!

Undoubtedly the most imaginative of the camp's projects was the formation of a motor club. This was the brainchild of one Tom Swallow, and as a car enthusiast and motor engineer I was one of the forty founder members. Notes of talks given at our meetings were so meticulously written up, and to such a high standard, that in the late 1980s, when a facsimile edition was published as *The Fly-Wheel* it found worldwide favour.

All such benign activities aside, however, the German conviction that aircrew were high escape risks was not without foundation. Indeed, in late spring 1944 we had a tunnel which was already beyond the outer perimeter wire when a loaded sewage cart broke through the surface. What initially puzzled us was that the Germans seemed more concerned than angry. Especially when, within days they distributed pamphlets advising, 'The escape from prison camps is no longer a sport!' and explaining that with German resources being so hard pressed, escapers were far more likely to be shot now than ever before.

All became clear when we learnt of the tunnel escape from Stalag Luft Three, when a random fifty out of the seventy-plus escapers had been summarily executed. Certainly, having been high on our own exit draw, this gave me a lot to think about.

Stalag 4B's tunnel enterprise may have been a failure, but some months later our escape committee were to pull off a coup which it would have been difficult to match.

The circumstances were that, before the war, the widowed mother of one of our POWs, a Winston Barrington, had married a German and taken her husband's nationality. Having arrived in Stalag 4B, Winston had managed to contact his mother who then moved to nearby Muhlberg to be close to him. Since then Winston had been able to meet her, after swapping uniforms with one of the soldiers detailed to collect Red Cross parcels from the railway station.

In the wider world, meanwhile, the Soviet westerly advance was gathering pace. But

Returning POWs board Stirling transports at Brussels during Operation Exodus.

gathering both pace and substance were reports of their treatment of women. As the Soviets neared Muhlberg, therefore, it was decided that Winston's mother should be smuggled into the camp for safekeeping.

To accomplish this, the Red Cross party took out with them an extra uniform, then surrounded the lady as they brought their wagon back inside. 'Pete', as the lady now became, was then conveyed to prepared quarters beneath the stage of the theatre. And there she stayed, her presence unsuspected by all but a score or so POWs, finally emerging unmolested.

As a coda to this human vignette, over twenty years later, in 1968, at a POW-Association reunion in Edinburgh, 'Pete' would be presented on the stage, and her story told, bringing tumultuous applause. 'And your son?' asked our former camp compère, Bill Ray. 'After the war,' she replied sadly, 'he emigrated to Canada and we lost touch.'

'You did indeed,' Bill agreed, 'but if you look behind you now…'

The first signs we actually saw of the Soviet advance had been an influx of prisoners forced-marched from more eastern camps. After that, though, as the sounds of battle became daily more distinct, the guards became uneasy, even panicky.

On the night of 22 April 1945 we turned in as always. We were awoken by shooting and shouting during the night, but that also had become commonplace, so after peering out and seeing nothing, we went back to sleep. At 0800 hours we had begun shuffling out for the obligatory roll call when the shout went up, 'There're no Jerries in the boxes!' We saw then that the Germans had decamped overnight! Without a by-your-leave. And after all that time!

Shortly afterwards three Russian horsemen appeared, gave the camp the once-over, and rode off. Later a Russian officer arrived and told us not to venture outside the wire. His men, he told us, would supply us with all the food we needed. Then he disappeared, and that was the last we were to see of him, or his promised food.

A day or so later, more Russians arrived. And that food? 'Do what we do,' they told

us, 'live off the land.'

Eventually, fed up with waiting, a party of us went into Muhlberg and simply commandeered what we needed. There was little enough, so the live rabbit I found in a shed was particularly prized.

Our next visitors were a jeepload of Americans, simply bristling with readied weapons of every type and

Americans and Russians meet at Torgau.

calibre. 'We know you're here,' they assured us, 'so just sit tight and we'll get you out.'

Some time later, an RAF jeep rolled up, its flight lieutenant passenger packing only a holstered pistol. But with the same, by now hackneyed, reassurance: the RAF had things in train to liberate us, but he was unable to say when, so have patience, chaps ...

I truly believe this was the last straw; this notion that the RAF were organising things! Just the same, we continued to sit. After all, leaving was fraught with danger, as we had discovered when foraging in Muhlberg, with trigger-happy Russians everywhere.

We knew by then, however, that the Americans were not far off, having met up with the Russians at Torgau. Finally, twenty-four hours later, five of us decided to set off. My old crewmates, Freddie and Dick elected to stay put and wait. As for us five, having made the decision, getting our kit together took barely ten minutes. Nor did we spare a backward glance for our home-from-home of very nearly two years. Instead, taking a bearing, we simply headed north.

Our journey, if fraught at times, paid off. Reaching the Americans, we then made our way to Brussels, arriving in time for VE Day and to be flown home by the RAF.

For an interminable thirty-six hours we were probed by the medics in Cosford's RAF hospital. When I finally arrived home, to be vociferously greeted at the gate by my old dog, Sandy, and to see awaiting me not only mum and dad, but behind them Betty, I could scarcely credit that it was a bare eight days since I had walked from the compound of Stalag 4B.

Sandy Slack, early 2010.

I had arrived home on 12 May 1945 but the demobilisation process did not release me for another year. During that time I had several postings, but in the September married Betty.

My final attachment was to Newton, just outside Nottingham, where I was able to scrounge a nostalgic flight in an Oxford. But this was a far cry from the Halifax, and I realised, not without a little regret, that my flying days were over. On 12 June 1946, therefore, I reported to the White City Stadium, near Shepherd's Bush, in London, chose a sports jacket and flannels rather than a de-mob suit, and just minutes later emerged, a civilian, anxious to get home to Betty and to my new life.

Although I returned to my old firm as a motor engineer, my interests had widened and in 1965 Betty and I set up our own firm, marketing hosiery, a business we happily pursued for twenty-five years until 1988 when we decided to retire – a retirement in which Service-linked activities have figured largely.

In 1968, during a commemorative dinner given by the Caterpillar Club [see Glossary], a group of us decided to form the Stalag 4B ex-Prisoner of War Association. This proved very successful and among other activities over the years saw some of us returning to Muhlberg in 2001.

Entering the reconstructed gates we learnt that the Soviets had used it to incarcerate an estimated 11,000 German Army prisoners, only 4,000 of whom were known to have been released. Not until forty-one years after that, when the Soviets left, was it possible to erect a memorial.

By the time of that visit, however, with anno domini creeping up, we had already declared our 2005 meeting to be the last.

But then, who knows!

Founder members of the Stalag 4B Motor Club, 1988.

2

Jamming the Night-Fighters

Flight Lieutenant Frederick G. James, DFC
Pilot

My flying career began with a setback. At the aircrew selection centre at Cardington they had established that I was both fit enough and keen enough for aircrew. However, as my maths paper had not met the grade for pilot or navigator, I had been assessed as suitable for training either as a wireless operator or as a flight engineer. Having mulled this over I had written to the Air Ministry to say that I was cramming to improve my maths. Born doubters, they replied that they needed proof, at which I had approached the maths master at Bakewell's Lady Manner's School who set me a test, then forwarded the results. So it was that when I returned to the selection centre I was accepted as a pilot, joining the RAF on 10 December 1940.

My initial posting was to Lord's Cricket Ground, a venue which struck me as ironic, a boyhood ambition having been to play for England and at Lord's. Here I was, being called upon to play for England, but at a game that bore no resemblance to cricket, and at a Lord's that had become No. 1 Aircrew Reception Centre (ACRC), or more informally, 'Number One Arsey Darsey'.

After kitting out, the next stop was the Initial Training Wing at Torquay where we did our square-bashing and began to learn the rudiments of our new trades.

At this time much of the flying training was being done overseas, in the Dominions and the still-neutral United States, not least to take advantage of the continuity afforded by the good weather. My posting was to the States.

The Atlantic crossing to Halifax, Nova Scotia, was uneventful, after which we were taken by train into the USA, to Maxwell Field, Alabama, my clearest memory of the trip being a luxury meal enjoyed on the roll. Our three weeks at Maxwell Field were spent 'acclimatising', which meant more square-bashing as well as continuing with lectures. But it was not all work, for we had the weekends to ourselves.

To a man we had been issued with double-breasted grey suits from the Fifty-Shilling Tailors, which might as well have been a uniform, so that on a Sunday morning you could pick out an RAF cadet anywhere. We'd go to church and hope – invariably successfully – to be taken home for a meal. 'We just love you British boys,' folk would say, 'you come home to lunch with us.'

To begin the primary stage of our flying training we were moved to Albany, Georgia, to fly the Boeing Stearman, a biplane trainer. I proved to be a slow starter and took a lengthy eleven hours to go solo. I can now see that this was largely because I did not get on with my instructor: essentially he shocked me by his shouting and his coarseness. 'You son of a bitch' was the mildest of his mouthings. Eventually, as the hours ticked on, I was sent for a flight commander's check. He proved a different type altogether and immediately put me at my ease. Certainly, having had me fly him around for a while, he indicated that I land, clambered out and clapped me on the shoulder.

'I'm sending you solo,' he bawled over the engine note, 'not because you think you're ready, but because I know you are.'

It was a heartening admonition that sank deep and one I was to use to good effect during my post-war teaching career. But back then, in Georgia, I duly went solo on 10 December 1941, a year to the day after I joined up. The tenth, again…

During my stay in America I flew three types of aircraft. For the primary stage, as I have said, the Stearman. Next, at the basic stage, the Vultee Valiant BT-13, in which instructor and pupil sat in tandem beneath a shared canopy. The Vultee was also equipped with blind-flying instruments so that, among other things, we were shown the basics of flying in foul weather, being hooded during those exercises to ensure that we had to depend upon our instruments. Finally there was the Harvard, similar in appearance to the Vultee, which we flew throughout the advanced stage.

We did a certain amount of night flying, and many cross-countries, largely flying in fair weather over reasonably level terrain utterly uncomplicated by industrial clutter. Finally, having completed the whole course, we received our RAF wings and sergeant's stripes. Beyond that, the expectation was that a flight sergeant's crown would follow a year later, with warrant officer status in a further twelve months, except that I had been commissioned by then.

Once back in the United Kingdom I was posted to No. 11 Operational Training Unit (OTU) at RAF Bassingbourn, Cambridgeshire. The function of this unit was to get us ready for operational flying, the first step being to form us into crews. This was done by the seemingly haphazard method of having pilots and crews self-select each other; just the same, most crews gelled nicely.

Having crewed up, we were introduced to the Vickers Wellington, doing most of our flying from Bassingbourn's satellite airfield, Steeple Morden. Then, in late 1942, when the Americans pushed us out of Bassingbourn, the unit went to Westcott, near Aylesbury, where we again flew from the main station's satellite, in this case, Oakley.

A Vickers Wellington.

The flying syllabus got us thoroughly used to the Wellington, with sorties which variously exercised each crew member, although, of course, the pilots and navigators were always involved. I must say that it went swimmingly – until it came to our final night-flying cross-country.

We duly got airborne. Even at briefing, though, the weather had not seemed all that promising, so it came as no real surprise to find that by the time we turned onto the final leg the weather at Oakley had begun closing in – for now, home from the States, we were back to good old British fog and low cloud! But weather threatening to clamp down merely meant that the pressure was on. Aircraft were in short supply and sorely needed back at base, and near-trained as we were, we were expected to pull out all the stops. But to have attempted to return to Oakley that night would have been foolhardy. I therefore called 'Darky', the emergency get-you-home service [see Glossary].

Darky came up trumps, recommending a westerly heading for the nearest airfield where conditions were acceptable for landing. So it was with an easier mind that I settled onto the new course.

I shall never know what actually went wrong. Undoubtedly I was flying too low. And quite likely the pressure acting on the altimeter had changed while we had been airborne, for in those days we would set the needle to read zero on take-off, and then leave it: we might get an updated pressure setting on returning from long ops, but certainly not as a matter of course.

Whatever the underlying reason, though, what with the darkness and the cloud, I was caught out by a pylon on a hilltop, the aircraft striking catastrophically and disintegrating. I was thrown clear, banging my head and injuring my shin. But my bomb aimer, a New Zealander, positioned in the nose station ready to map-read, was killed instantly.

At the court of inquiry, the meteorological people explained that a bad-weather front had swept across the region far more quickly than expected; additionally that the winds associated with it had been far stronger than those given to my crew. Despite this, however, and although two other training Wellingtons had been lost that night, the overall finding was that the three crashes had been due to errors of judgement in navigation!

The court of inquiry came later, of course. In part, they had to wait until I was fit enough to appear, for after the crash I had remained pretty well unconscious for almost ten days. And hardly any wonder, for on coming to I learnt that a civilian doctor had come to the crash, taken a glance at me, decided I was past help and had turned away to attend to the others. For my part, when I first awoke in hospital I had found myself confronted by what I could only take for a white-coated angel.

Many years later, after the 1989 Kegworth M1 air crash I was to read that a traumatised by-chance-aider was paid £75,000 in compensation. Back in 1942, when the civilian doctor submitted a claim for his ruined suit, Air Ministry told him that as the RAF had not summoned him he was not entitled to compensation.

However, the moment my leg injury allowed me to travel I was dispatched to the Central Medical Establishment at Kelvin House in London to undergo brain tests: three of them. I don't doubt that the medics wanted to establish just how the head injury had affected my mental state, seeing that, despite the trauma of the crash and the death of my bomb aimer, I actually wanted to get back into the air!

But I forgot! The date of that crash? 10 December 1942. The *tenth*! The Glorious Tenth! Join up, first solo, and a major crash, all on the tenth! With so many more tenths to come, hopefully!

And yet ... on completion of the OTU course I had been scheduled for No. 75 Squadron, and Stirlings: death traps, as many thought. In the event I finished up on a Lancaster squadron. So without the intervention of that seemingly special date, how many more tenths would an operational tour on Stirlings have afforded me?

Thankfully, there was little time for morbid reflections, for while recovering from my injuries I was employed in the station's Airmanship Hall, supervising crash-landing drills and ditching procedures on a Wellington fuselage, organising dinghy drills and discussing parachute-landing techniques. In the course of time, however, I was passed fit to fly again, and after a refresher course on Oxfords at Caistor, a satellite of Cranwell, I was sent to No. 1521 Beam Approach Training Unit at Stradishall, in Suffolk, to learn about bad-weather approaches.

The first step was to sort out the complexities of the beam-approach procedure in the Link Trainer, after which we turned to airborne training, flying in daylight and keeping our eyes on the flight instruments while interpreting the signals in the headset. Having manoeuvred ourselves to be facing towards the airfield it was a matter of getting onto the centre line. This involved passing through a zone of either dots or dashes, negotiating a mushy zone in which you heard both dots and dashes, and finally of gingerly edging over to find the steady signal of the actual beam.

Once we'd got ourselves onto the exact centre-line we'd then descend to 600 feet, holding that height until we received the Outer Marker signal. At that, and with wheels and flaps down, we'd lose height gradually to the Inner Marker, which was right on the edge of the airfield. At this final signal, we'd look up. If we could see the runway, we'd land. But if we'd drifted off the centre-line or if the visibility was too bad to see the runway, we'd climb away and go to an airfield where conditions were better.

As it happened, I was to do two beam-approach courses but only once to actually use – or, at least, partially use – the beam in anger. That was on a night when, having left the target, we picked up so much ice that we were unable to maintain height over the North Sea. As we neared base we were down to 2,000 feet and still in cloud. Even so I did not formally call for permission to carry out a full beam approach for despite the fact that I'd come away from both beam-courses with above-average ratings the procedure

The Link Trainer, with the desk-top crab recorder inking in the track flown.

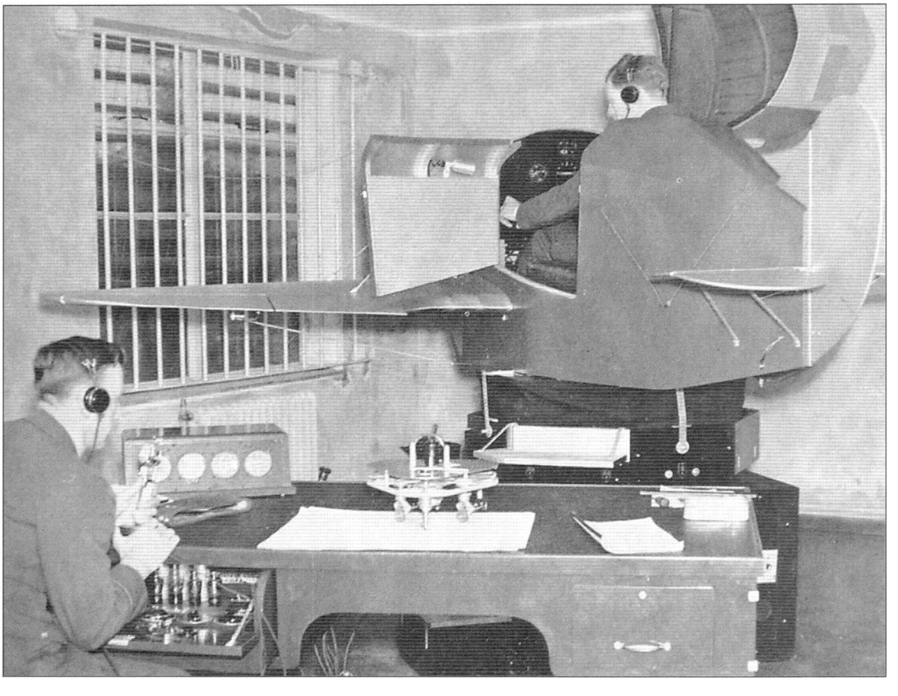

A Lancaster of No. 101 Squadron: the two vertical Airborne Cigar (jamming) aerials are forward of the turret.

was always fraught. On that occasion, moreover, there were returning aircraft homing in from all directions so although we lined up using the beam, on breaking cloud we kept our eyes and ears open, saw the lights and landed visually.

But that came later, whereas the beam courses at Stradishall and Cranwell had been followed by another Wellington OTU, this one at Castle Donington. The course itself was straightforward enough, but the aircraft were clapped out from overuse so that when we lost an engine and were forced to land on only one it surprised nobody. We battled on, however, the final sortie being a leaflet drop over Occupied France: my first op!

* * *

My next move was to No. 1662 Heavy Conversion Unit at Blyton, near Gainsborough, Lincolnshire, to fly the Halifax as an introduction to four-engined aircraft. I did not like this machine at all. But then came the Lancaster Finishing School at Hemswell. And I remember telling myself, 'I'm here at last: in the number one seat in the RAF!'

Finally operational, I was posted to No. 101 Squadron, a specialist radio-countermeasures unit whose Lancasters were fitted with equipment dedicated to jamming the control instructions transmitted to German fighters. To do the jamming we carried an eighth crew member, a special-operations man (the SO), a German speaker, who used a piece of equipment codenamed Airborne Cigar (ABC).

Externally this comprised two 7-foot aerials on the fuselage, another below the bomb-aimer's window, and a shorter aerial nearer the tail. Internally, a combination of a receiver and three, 50-watt T3160-type transmitters was employed. A blip on the cathode ray tube of a scanning device would indicate a voice signal. If the SO recognised a German fighter-director broadcast, he would jam it with the first transmitter, sweeping on after that to block two more, the No.101 Squadron contingent between them jamming virtually the whole spectrum.

The SO's windowless station was just aft of the main spar on the port side. He was further isolated by having his intercom switched off so that crew exchanges would not distract. In case of need, however, the pilot could use a red attention-getter light.

My first SO was Pilot Officer Keith Gosling who, being the only other officer on the crew, I grew quite pally with. After a few ops, however, he was detailed to fill in on a Ruhr trip with another crew, and as the aircraft failed to return, I completed my tour with Sergeant Roy Hall.

When on operations, our squadron's aircraft would be strung out in pairs along the bomber stream, as many as twenty-seven of them at times. This, of course, was to ensure that the cover to any part of the stream was maintained should one of a pair be shot down. Apart from that, we acted as normal units of the main force, although the weight of the ABC equipment and the extra crew member reduced our bomb load by 1,000 pounds.

We were stationed at Ludford Magna, east of Market Rasen on the southern end of the Lincolnshire Wolds, 400 feet above sea level, an airfield that was nearly always in the clear when we arrived back from ops. On the odd foggy occasion we diverted to Woodbridge, in Suffolk, or Manston, in Kent, where they had the very effective FIDO installed (Fog, Investigation and Dispersal Operation). FIDO, it will be recalled, used burning petrol alongside the runway to disperse the fog, the flames additionally acting as a visual beacon.

In the States we had done very little instrument-flying training, and not that much more after our return. But now, flying at night and over the wartime blackout, I got quite

A Lancaster landing with the aid of FIDO.

accustomed to it, using the turn and bank as a major aid. In fact, we got a lot of practice, for on ops we tended to fly manually. 'George' – our automatic pilot – was all very well in the normal way of things but disengaging it meant losing valuable seconds which might be better spent in beginning an evasion manoeuvre. A trivial matter, perhaps, but it certainly paid off on the night of 22 June 1944 when we attacked the marshalling yards at Reims.

The ten-minute run-up to the target was obscured by cloud. This forced us to do an orbit, always an unwelcome procedure, but one which, on this occasion, gave the target markers time to re-mark, so that on actually running-up we were able to drop our bombs with confidence. Having done so, it was necessary to hold the course for a prescribed time to obtain an aiming-point photo, but shortly after turning away Ken Gibbs, the mid-upper gunner, warned that two fighters were closing fast.

Between them they set the starboard engine on fire and sprayed both tail- and nose-turret areas. George Williams, from the tail, reported that although his turret had been hit, he was OK. Ron Davies, the bomb aimer, had an even closer escape. Having pre-selected the bomb switches he had then moved to the front turret for the run-in. Later, tracing out the damage pattern, it became obvious that had I not skidded immediately, or wasted even a millisecond in disengaging the auto pilot, he would have caught a fair old packet.

With the fighters gone – virtually all we saw of them was their tracer – I cut the fuel, stopped and feathered the engine, and operated the fire extinguisher. And wonder of wonders, the fire went out!

Now on three engines we swiftly became a very lame duck. The necessity to do an orbit had already put us to the rear of the stream and from then on we steadily fell further behind. This meant, of course, that as we approached the sea, the enemy coastal defences, both searchlights and guns, were able to concentrate all their ill will on us. I seemed to be forever winging over first one way and then the other in evasive corkscrews, but eventually things went quiet and we knew that we had won clear. So far, at least.

There was more of interest to come, however, for limping back, with nerves tense and every eye alert, we were mystified when two fiery flares appeared from nowhere and streaked on ahead. Belatedly we realised that these were the exhausts of two V1 pulse-jet Flying Bombs! Interesting indeed – to the Intelligence people, though. Our major concern was where to put down.

We considered heading for the crash airfield at Woodbridge but eventually decided to let 'Darky' make the decision for us. Answering our call the listening posts duly pointed us down the coast to Thorney Island, near Portsmouth, which obligingly marked itself by a cone of searchlights. Deliberately flying into these non-threatening beams we were intrigued on looking upwards to see a ghostly Lancaster clearly projected on the upper cloud!

But our night was not over yet, for on selecting the undercarriage down we got an unlocked indication for one of the wheels. When I closed the throttles as a test, however, the warning horn did not blow, which suggested that the problem lay with the warning-light circuitry and not the undercarriage itself. On the other hand when we lowered the flaps the aircraft swung markedly to port, from which we deduced that in putting paid to the starboard engine the fighters had also jammed the starboard flaps.

Nor were we to be afforded the luxury of the runway, for just then control came up to advise that a landing Mosquito had finished up in the sea, but not before strewing debris in its wake. They directed, therefore, that we should land on the grass to the right of the runway. Fair enough in itself, except that following touchdown I was unable to keep the aircraft straight: a cannon shell, it transpired, had punctured the starboard tyre. And perhaps we had lost even more bits than we knew, for some time later a Lancaster escape hatch was washed up nearby.

As for us, we returned to base by train. For my part, I suppose I should have been glad that it had all happened on the twenty-second of June, and not on my nemesis date, the tenth of December.

Shortly afterwards I finished my tour of operations. At that time, the length of an operational tour had been fixed at thirty-five bombing sorties but I ended up doing thirty-

The crew: (left to right) *Sergeant Ron Davies, bomb aimer; Sergeant Paddy Orr, flight engineer; Sergeant George ('Titch') Taylor, wireless operator/air gunner; Sergeant George Williams, rear gunner, Royal Canadian Air Force (RCAF); Frederick G. James, DFC, pilot; Sergeant Jim Coleman, navigator, RCAF; Flying Officer Ken Gibbs, DFC, mid-upper gunner; Sergeant Roy Hall, special operations operator.*

six. Then again we had been forced to turn back from two other ops, once due to low oil pressure and a second time after the rear turret had stopped working.

I was not to rest long, however, for I was soon recalled to operations, this time to Coastal Command where one of my jobs was to check the accuracy of bombsights on moving targets. After a spell there I was then moved to yet another command, to Transport Command, where I flew Dakotas from RAF Wymeswold. The dear old Dakota, the only RAF aircraft in which people were legally permitted to smoke!

The Distinguished Flying Cross (DFC), broad purple and white diagonals.

The war came to an end, and it was time to face the future. Having amassed about a thousand hours in the air, and having had Transport Command experience, I applied to Derby Aviation for a job (Derby Aviation, subsequently British Midland Airways, later BMI, later still part of Lufthansa!). However, there were so many pilots seeking employment that there seemed no hope, so, possibly aided by the boning-up I'd done to get into the pilot's seat, I trained as a maths teacher under the Emergency Training Scheme, eventually turning full circle with a job at the very establishment where I had been mentored for the RAF entrance exam, Lady Manner's School in Bakewell.

Some months before, though, at the teachers' training college, my recent past had caught up with me. I was advised that a package awaited me in the admin office. The admin office! No Buckingham Palace, no king, no future queen. Just a junior clerk to hand me a box containing my Distinguished Flying Cross. But then awards are a sore point for so many of us. For despite all the operations they flew my crew were

The Aircrew Europe Star, thin yellow outer strips enclose a black-edged light blue ribbon (3 September 1939 up to 5 June 1944).

not even entitled to the Aircrew Europe Star! Which meant that none of them had anything to set them apart from airmen – though worthy in their own right – who had never flown, and helps explain why there is so much bitterness that no Bomber Command medal was ever struck.

But perhaps the offhand award was a portent of things to come. For when the years went by and it was time for me to retire from the school, a Lancaster flypast was laid on as a surprise. A delightful gesture! Only it had been kept so secret, even from Myfanwy, my wife, that we missed it.

I have touched upon the bitterness surrounding the post-war lack of recognition for Bomber Command, and the stigma that has been attached to the Command's policy, largely by after-the-event rationalists – largely, though not entirely, of course, for there were genuine wartime dissenters too. But on that head I point questioners towards the majority British view one came upon in the 1940s, the view almost universally expressed when the only way of striking back at the enemy was by flying over his territory and carrying the war to him.

As for the stresses imposed upon those undertaking the task, I have often been asked about my emotions during those days. I respond by saying that what is now seen by some as a moral issue hardly weighed then. We were all well aware of what had happened to countless cities from Warsaw to Wallasey. And there was a war to be won.

And yet, a poignant revelation awaited me. When my first SO, Pilot Officer Keith

Gosling, had failed to return, we'd fatalistically accepted that he'd got the chop. It transpired, however, that it had not been that simple. His pilot on that fill-in trip had been a Pilot Officer Meier, RCAF, and of German extraction. Having bombed the target, and although the aircraft was undamaged, Meier later claimed that he unsuccessfully tried to persuade the crew that bombing was morally wrong. Certainly, the bomb aimer was either ordered to bale out, or decided to – his account varied – and successfully evaded. But twenty minutes later, Meier seems to have put the aircraft into a banked dive, and jumped himself, leaving the other six crew, including Keith, to crash and burn.

Meier became a POW, but in 1945, when his fellow POWs were forced-marched westwards, he disappeared, re-appearing years later in East Germany seeking to be allowed back to Canada. The Canadian authorities, having investigated the case, became embarrassed, and continually stood him off until 1977, when he died, finally reckoning him among those of their black sheep who were 'deemed never to have served'. And so we learnt that Keith and his fellow crew members might well have fallen victim to their pilot's flawed moral conscience.

The moral aspect of bombing aside, however, those who are familiar with the period far more often ask about the fear. Yet I have had to be honest and reply that I was never afraid during operations, not even on the worst of them. Nor did we, as a crew, discuss the perils we faced, and fortunately so many of us survived and kept in touch that I have

Another flyover, 6 September 2009, commemorating the three-year tenure of No. 1 ACRC: Aircrew Reception Centre, Lord's Cricket Ground.

The human cost of carrying the war home ...

been able to double-check this. For instance, on the two occasions when technicalities forced us to abort the operation – which meant that to count towards our tour the sortie would have to be done again – we talked over the problem between us so that the decision to turn back and face it all again was unanimous.

On the other hand, after our first Lancaster op our orginal mid-upper gunner went off to the squadron office, and simply disappeared. At the time we assumed he had received one of those out-of-the-blue wartime postings They happened. Ops aside, people were there and then they weren't. Besides, before we really had time to notice the loss, third-tour veteran Ken Gibbs, DFC, joined us as a replacement. It was only after the war that the penny dropped and we realised that the first op had simply been too much for our gunner, that having admitted to this in the office he would have been hurried off the station and subsequently branded with the iniquitous term 'lack of moral fibre' (the acronym was LMF).

Frederick James in 2010

I have to admit, though, that when alone in bed, fear would indeed visit me. And it could well be, of course, that the fear us youngsters did not feel was felt by others on our behalf. My parents later told me that whenever they heard the BBC announce that so many of our aircraft had failed to return they would sit on tenterhooks, expecting a knock on the door. Not only that, but my mother, suddenly noticing that my father was no longer in the room, would find him at the gate, looking along the road to see if the policeman was coming with a message...

Certainly there had been grounds enough for such concern. Between 18 November 1943 and 24 March 1944 our own unit, No. 101 Squadron, lost seventeen aircraft. Our host station, RAF Ludford Magna, lost a total of 113 of its Lancasters.

With regard to our crew, bomb aimer Ron Davies was still in touch in 2010, but tail-end-charlie George Williams, from Canada, and wireless operator/air gunner George Taylor, both died in 2009. Navigator Jim Coleman passed on some years earlier, while our special-operations operator, Roy Hall, who had flown as a wireless operator before taking on the SO job and had been commissioned after leaving us, died in 2007.

As for mid-upper gunner Ken Gibbs, DFC – well into his third tour when he joined us – he had aspired to fly a hundred ops. On leaving us he flew on. Only to be shot down and killed on his ninety-seventh op.

As I have said, no obvious feelings of fear back then, but these days I get this dream, always the same scenario. I am scheduled for ops once more. I duly find my way to the aircraft. And my crew are there. Not, however, as I last saw them, just a few of them, at some latter-day reunion. But all eight of them. And just as they were then. Not a day older. Only I have aged. Only I am frightened. Only I am alone. And when I awake, I think back and wonder how, all those years ago, we ever managed to handle the fear that had to have been there.

3

The Wind Finders

Flight Lieutenant Phil Tetlow
wireless operator/air gunner

While I was working for Marconi I was in a reserved occupation and couldn't be called up, although when the Air Training Corps came into being in February 1941 I was one of its original members. Later, however, it became permissible to volunteer to fly with the RAF, so shortly after turning seventeen, I did just that.

Although disappointed to be told that a slight squint in one eye disbarred me from pilot training, I was delighted to be accepted as a wireless operator-cum-air gunner; far too delighted, indeed, to ask why a squint should hinder a pilot but not a gunner! Even then I had to wait until I was eighteen before starting training but I filled my spare time with fire-watching duties for the ARP (Air Raid Precautions) until, in August 1942, I reported to Blackpool for initial service training.

The course did introduce various flight-related topics but much of our time was spent being harried by corporal drill instructors who seemed to have a particular down on prospective aircrew. Indeed, throughout my service I was to be conscious of the additional gulf set up at that time between fliers and non-fliers, for the latter – whom in our youthful arrogance we dubbed 'Penguins' – might spend ten years rising to the rank of sergeant whereas fliers could be given that status, with all its privileges, in less than as many months. Not only that, but having got the rank, aircrew received an additional seven shillings a day flying pay! Just the same, after the sixteen months it took me to get my three stripes I really felt I'd earned them.

Course followed course. At Blackpool we had become proficient at foot drill and had been introduced to the morse code and, more pleasingly, to the fact that even the trainee-aircrew sidecap flash acted as a magnet to the girls! At Yatesbury, in Wiltshire, we spent four months on radio theory, also achieving the required morse speed of twenty words a minute. We also guarded the blacked-out white horse – yes, it really was blacked out, for security! – on the hill above the camp; and successfully so, for to the best of my knowledge it is there yet. But after Yatesbury, and with our wireless badges on our right arms, there was a two-month hiatus, with too many trainee aircrew blocking the system. Rather than kick my heels, I grasped at the chance to move to No.15 (Pilots) Advanced Flying Unit at Greenham Common, near Newbury, where they had Airspeed Oxfords. Not only did I get airborne for the first time myself, but I got my eye in, building up over thirty hours of flying time.

In June 1943, however, I resumed training at No. 4 Radio School at Madley, near Hereford, practising airborne wireless operating in de Havilland Dominie biplanes and Percival Proctors. Operating a morse key in such light aircraft was difficult enough as it was, but the staff pilots were resting from ops and tended to get bored with such docile cab-driving, far preferring to low-fly despite our protestations that to get our wireless contacts we needed a fair bit of height. Soldiering through this lack of co-operation, in September 1943 we qualified as wireless operators (air) and entrained to No.10 Air Gunnery School at Walney Island, near Barrow-in-Furness.

During the next six weeks we were taught air gunnery, again by resting fliers, some of whom – not least those showing burn scars – brought home to us just what achieving our goal of brevet and stripes might mean. We were not dissuaded, however, and our instructors' insistence that the really hard times for the bomber force were over, and the general feeling that the war could not have long to run, merely spurred us on.

And finally, on 13 November 1943, a fully qualified wireless operator air gunner (Wop/AG) at last, I spent the evening sewing on my sergeant's stripes, and even more proudly, the long-coveted AG brevet.

Even now, there was more training to come, so that, what with odd detachments during backlog delays, it was January 1944 before I arrived at Silverstone, at No. 17 Operational Training Unit, to join a crew.

Air-gunner in an Oxford turret, firing at a drogue towed by a Fairey Battle.

Standing, left to right: Sergeant Pete Ramwell, bomb aimer; Sergeant Phil Tetlow, wireless operator/air gunner; Flying Officer Don Macintosh, pilot; Sergeant Nigel Hawkins, navigator; Sergeant Bob Cosser, flight engineer. Front row: Sergeant Jock Wood, mid-upper gunner; Sergeant Geoff Owen, rear gunner.

Crewing up was done by self-selection, a process which smacked of the cattle market. The pilots, I gathered – the aircraft captains – had some notion of how the rest of us had done on our courses, but we had no such yardstick to apply when allying ourselves to the men who would so directly hold our lives in their hands. So how to choose?

As it happened, I had met a bomb aimer, Pete Ramwell, who now recommended me to a tall, gangling Scottish pilot named Donald Macintosh, a former Glasgow policeman. What Sergeant Mac saw as he eyed me I cannot say, but although he accepted me I was never to feel any real rapport between us. That being said, he was to prove an excellent pilot and captain.

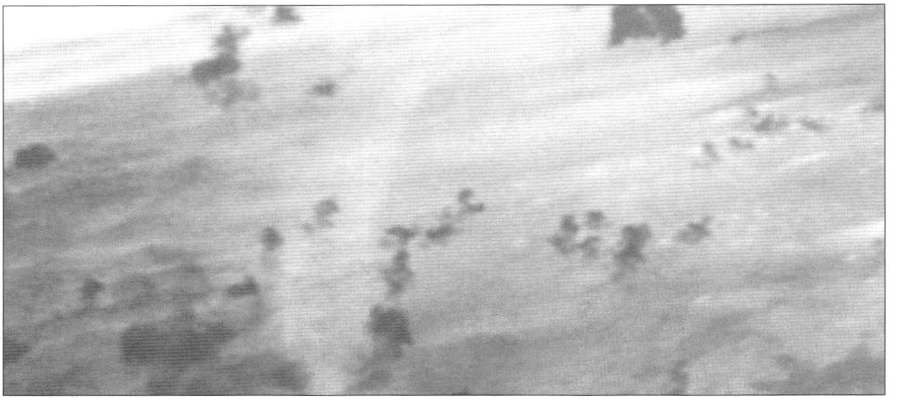

We saw some distant flak...

It was also to transpire that he was very competitive, always wanting his crew to be best. Which was fine by me, as far as it went. It would take far longer to discover that he also had a hidden agenda!

So it was that, senior NCOs all, we came together to learn to fly, initially, the Vickers Wellington bomber. There was Mac, the pilot and captain. Then there was Nigel (Nije) Hawkins, an Oxford graduate, a brilliant mathematician, and a great navigator. If he was forever to stand rather aloof at least he could work well with Mac!

There was also my bomb-aimer acquaintance, Pete Ramwell, from Macclesfield. He aspired to be an architect yet, ironically, had just become qualified to destroy architecture! Next in the hierarchy was me, with my dual role of wireless operator and air gunner.

After that there were our air gunners, each wearing the AG brevet like me, but not qualified to wear the wireless flash. The first, Geoff Owen, a mouthy Yorkshireman, took over the rear turret. The other, Ian (Jock) Wood, destined to occupy the mid-upper turret when we got onto heavies, was a dour former gamekeeper; another Scot, a natural shot and, at twenty-three, the oldest member of the crew. A seemingly dysfunctional bunch, yet we passed out top of the course.

The prize for doing so was to fly as a diversion for a real raid, penetrating deep into France, to Orleans, photographing a designated target and showering out propaganda leaflets and radar-distracting Window. We saw some distant flak but in the main we occupied ourselves with trying to keep warm and in sampling our boxed sandwiches and Horlicks tablets, and our coffee flasks.

There was a sting in the tail, however, when the Portsmouth defences opened up on us. We were unscathed but still shaken when we landed. Only to be greeted with howls of laughter: 'Oh, that's the navy, they're always trigger happy.'

We were then posted to No. 1654 Heavy Conversion Unit, at Wigsley, near Lincoln, essentially to enable the pilot and a new crew member, the flight engineer, to gain experience on four-engined bombers; in this case, the Short Stirling. Our assigned flight engineer cracked his skull during our first sortie but we quickly settled with his replacement, Bob Cosser, a qualified farm-equipment engineer. At twenty-eight he

A 4,000 pound blockbuster, or cookie.

usurped Jock Wood as the oldest of the crew, and although not given to verbosity was as generous as they come.

There was another delay, this time due to lack of aircraft, before we were accepted by No. 5 Lancaster Finishing School at Syerston, near Nottingham. But after seven weeks we were finally introduced to, and began to get familiar with, the justly-celebrated bomber. Three weeks we were allocated, and little enough time at that. Again Mac pushed us to do well, but then he did well himself when on an early sortie we lost first our starboard-inner engine and then our port outer, despite which he brought us to a safe landing, earning himself a green endorsement for a job well done. And perhaps it all helped, for when it came to postings we were able to make our choice.

Despite the ubiquitous 'Careless Talk Costs Lives' posters, pub gossip had advised us that No. 9 Squadron was soon to become a special-duties squadron. Accordingly, Mac successfully nominated this as our first choice.

No. 9 Squadron was stationed at Bardney, ten miles east of Lincoln, the accommodation being Nissen huts, all very spartan, with curved, corrugated-iron walls, a central coke-fired stove, a bare concrete floor, a trestle table, four folding chairs, and beds and lockers for the seven of us. And it was still the seven of us, for although, as a four-engined captain, Mac became an instant flying officer he continued to spend a lot of time with us.

Our respective leaders (signals, bombing, gunnery, navigation) spent some time explaining how their sections worked and interlinked. The highlight of our 'arrival' however, came when we found ourselves in the presence of our very own Lancaster, bandbox-new out of the factory. Swiftly naming it *Cock o' the North*, we had the groundcrew paint a cockerel with a bomb in its claws. We also decided that for each of our ops we'd add a tiny bomb symbol.

What peace of mind it might have given us to know that by the time we did our last flight as a crew there would be forty-two of these!

On 25 July 1944 we became truly operational, carrying out a daylight raid on St. Cyr, the French Military Academy to the west of Paris, then a German headquarters, barracks and communications centre. Peering through the astrodome my overriding memory of the sortie was the seeming inevitability of collision as 200 Lancasters milled about over the concentration area and gradually coalesced into a single stream.

Each aircraft carried a 4,000 pound blockbuster, or cookie – a finless, thin-cased bomb – and eight 1,000 pound high-explosive bombs, the whole force dropping within four minutes. Flak, I noted, was heavy and sustained, and our aircraft was holed several times. The older hands regarded this as a milk run, but it was certainly no milk run for the Lanc which went down just off to our right. And I remember that, as a crew, we had little enough to say at debriefing.

Left, the aerial (bottom projection) for the rearward-facing Monica radar; right, the scope: a poisoned chalice …

Our next op came two nights later, and was a different kettle of fish entirely, the target being Stuttgart. This time we knew the sky was full of aircraft, but we couldn't see them. What we could see, though, was the flak and the searchlights, the target indicators dropped by Pathfinder Force, and the fires on the ground below. Then, on the run-in we were stalked by a fighter, but I had seen him on our rearward-facing radar – codenamed Monica – and as I was able to tell Mac to corkscrew in evasion the enemy aircraft was unable to press home an attack. We landed eight hours after taking off, shaken and shattered, but this time making our debriefing report in a state approaching delirium.

Monica, as some only suspected at the time, would turn out to be a poisoned chalice, for it transpired that German fighters could actually home in on it! Dubious radar aids aside, however, there was little enough rest from then on. Though one op was fraught in a rather different way from the others. We had been assigned another crew's aircraft and dispatched to give close support to the army at Cahagnes in Normandy. Low cloud over the area meant that we had to abort our drop and jettison our bombs in the sea.

Only these had been incorrectly fused, so that they exploded, sending shrapnel rattling up into our undersurfaces.

We duly got back to Bardney, to be met by a furious owner-crew. The aircraft, lettered 'J', which they had named *Johnny Walker*, was approaching its one-hundredth op and they were on a promise of two crates of Johnny Walker whisky when it did so. Fortunately for us, our combined groundcrews pulled out all the stops – when didn't they? – so that 'J' successfully completed its one hundred, and the libation was duly received.

Eight ops, we did, in eleven days, some against V1 Flying Bomb installations, and mostly in daylight. Things, as everyone told us, had certainly changed with the Invasion! Then our aircraft became due for a major servicing. We were sent on leave, to be gratified to find, on our return, that the 'insider information' had been correct, and that the squadron was indeed to operate as a special-duties unit, and in co-operation with No. 617, the Dambusters Squadron; in co-operation, or, as we were often to feel, under the domination of... Certainly, my diary refers to No. 617 Squadron as 'our deadly rivals'.

We first exercised our special function on a raid against the submarine pens at La Rochelle's La Pallice docks. Previous raids had not even dented the immense concrete installations but No. 617's Lancasters had been modified to carry the new 12,000 pound Tallboy bombs. These were designed to breach the pens, after which 2,000 pound armour-piercing bombs would complete the destruction. Bombing accuracy was essential, and although a new and sophisticated bombsight had been developed it needed to be fed with the actual wind at dropping height. Our special-duties job was to provide that wind.

The technique we employed was that some of our aircraft, normally six, would fly in advance of the main stream. About forty miles from the target, Mac would pick out and nominate a ground feature some way ahead of us, although on occasion, over total cloud cover, a dropped flare would have to do. Pete, the bomb aimer, would then call when we were exactly overhead the location. At that, Nigel, at his nav's station, would record the reading on his Air Position Indicator (API) and start the timing. Mac would then fly a five-minute

A Tallboy bomb.

left-hand racetrack pattern as accurately as possible. Then, as this was completed, Nigel would take another API reading, the difference between the two allowing him to calculate the windspeed and direction. The other five aircraft, formating on us throughout, would have come up with their own winds, from which the mean wind would be taken. This would then be passed on to enable the individual bomb aimers in the main force to update their settings.

Being wind-finders, of course, we not only risked becoming specifically targeted during this manoeuvre but having lagged behind the main force we then had to make our own bombing run; double jeopardy, as it were. And the flak put up, on this occasion by the U-boat pens, would be venomous. But then we had, after all, volunteered for special duties.

Again, my diary records that it was only crew co-operation that got us clear after the drop, all of us combining to advise Mac as the flak closed in so that he could weave out of its way.

On our second visit the wind-finding procedure was refined with a whole wave of bombers carrying out the racetrack so that we were no longer singled out. This, however, did not save the Lancaster whose debris we flew through as we ran in. And disappointingly, next day's photo reconnaissance showed the concrete pens still unbreached.

A somewhat similar raid on Brest – the first of two planned – steeled us yet more. With the Allied armies virtually ringing the port, we arrived early in order to carry out our wind finding. But then main force, which we had expected to be slowly closing, came up to us before we had regained the run-in heading. By then we were buffeting through the thickest flak yet, but suddenly there were Lancasters angling in from our beam.

A warning from Jock, our mid-upper, allowed Mac to evade a machine immediately overhead with its bomb bay open and about to release its load. Hard upon that Geoff yelled an advisory that a nearby Lanc had lost its rear turret to a bomb dropped from the machine above it. And even on the run-in the gunners had to interrupt with collision warnings, nettling bomb-aimer Pete. Suffice to say that of the three aircraft our squadron lost we were almost certain that two had been involved in collisions or downed by having bombs dropped on them.

Memory heals, but my diary entry following that op brings it all back: *From the moment I saw the first burst of flak I was trembling with sheer terror and I was still in a cold sweat when we hit the English coast. ... the other squadron, No. 167 Squadron, was totally obscured by smoke from the flak...*

I also recorded that in the time before take-off on the return visit to Brest, *'the most inane jokes would result in shrieks of hysterical laughter'.*

Tension on that return visit was particularly high yet although we had to overfly the full

A Halifax gunner, showing how close the friendly bomb came.

breadth of the harbour defences to reach our particular target – a large merchantman – there was not a trace of flak. Which had to mean enemy fighters! Except that nothing happened. Not a blessed thing! We dropped our loads, and flew home. Only, if anything, I was more unsettled by that uncanny dearth of opposition than by the horrendous flak of the previous day.

In the next few weeks we became aware that the squadron was no longer being tasked for operations. Instead, our time was spent in carrying out intensive bombing practices. As a personal side issue, we also noticed that as Mac's crew we were getting airborne rather more often than the rest. This was only of minor concern, however, and swiftly forgotten in the buzz that intensified with the delivery of new Lancasters.

These were not only modified to take the 12,000 pound Tallboy and some equally lethal extra-capacity fuel tanks, but they had been stripped of mid-upper turrets and much of their protective armour plate, clearly to save weight. It was equally clear that weight saving equated to longer range. Speculation ran rife.

And then telephone lines went dead, and nobody could leave camp. Jock, our mid-upper was distraught. His turret had gone, and Geoff would not swap places with him no matter what was brewing. Then, on 6 September 1944, the whole lot of us – Jock and his fellow mid-upper gunners too – were coached across to Woodhall Spa, the lair of No. 617 Squadron, for the introductory part of a briefing which, in its entirety, would take forty-eight hours.

A concealing sheet was pulled off a landscape model showing sheer-sided mountains and watery inlets. And among a cluster of defensive vessels, a major ship, looming larger than life despite being modelled to scale. At which the whole room fairly seethed. It was, of course, *Tirpitz*.

'And you are going to sink her,' Air Vice-Marshal 'Cocky' Cochrane, commander of No. 5 Group, told us.

We knew that many attacks on *Tirpitz* had failed. Now we learnt from No. 617's commanding officer, Wing Commander 'Willie' Tait, that this massive German capital ship, a menace to our Russian convoys and therefore tying up Royal Naval resources, was lying in cliff-ringed, virtually impregnable Alta Fjord on the north-western coast of Norway. The fjord, as we could see, was well out of range of aircraft from the United Kingdom. So we were to fly to Yagodnic, near Archangel, in the Soviet Union, wait until the Norwegian weather was suitable, and then mount a raid.

We were told too, that because of the mountainous terrain, there was only one feasible direction of approach to *Tirpitz*, and that as a defensive smokescreen could cover the fjord within eight minutes we needed an element of surprise. We had already been briefed about the flak defences. But nobody seemed to know about local enemy fighter strengths.

A skeleton staff of groundcrew had already been positioned in Russia. Now, at just after 1900 hours on 11 September 1944 we followed on. With fuel tanks filled to the gunwales we lifted off, and initially holding low beneath the German radar cover, set heading to overfly Norway, Sweden and Finland, for Russia. Not too surprisingly the neutral Swedes let fly at us – if only with tracer shells – but the mere fact that they fired at all disturbed Jock. Seeing which I pointed out to him that, not having a turret, he need not have come along, earning myself a foot in the ribs. In fact, the arrangement was that the gunners would spell each other in the freezing cold of the rear turret.

As we progressed, crossing still-hostile Finland without opposition, so the cloud base forced us ever lower until, as we approached Archangel, we were down to 800 feet. Even then Yagodnic eluded us in the mist, nor did my written brief on Russian frequencies and signals-procedures help, so that when we eventually glimpsed three parked Lancasters and Mac made a stomach-wrenching turn to put us down on the grass alongside we were extremely low on fuel. Others had not been so lucky. Two had found a more distant airfield, but seven had run out of fuel and crash-landed or, at best, forced-landed on flat ground.

The Russians turned out to be friendly enough but despite a band and a banner reading, 'Welcome to the Glorious Fliers of the Royal Air Force', the most noteworthy welcome we received, tired as we were, was from the myriad bugs awaiting us in our bedding.

Four days later, on 15 September 1944, photo-reconnaissance reported clear skies over the fjord, following which the reduced force of twenty-seven Lancasters began getting airborne at 1015 hours. Our crew had been designated as one of the three wind-finders, and I was to pass on the mean wind.

Flak began to blotch the sky long before Alta Fjord came into sight, so that on our bombing run smoke generators were already beginning to obscure the target. Indeed, Pete was forced to use the flash of *Tirpitz's* guns as an aiming point! He did find, however, that he was able to follow the big bomb most of the way down, only for its explosion to be masked in smoke. But by then Mac was curling out between the flak bursts and heading back to Yagodnic, putting us down again seven hours after we had lifted off.

There was a fraught wait then, prolonged because bad weather prevented photo-reconnaissance photographs from being taken, but eventually Norwegian Resistance sources advised that *Tirpitz*, though damaged, was still afloat. On the plus side no aircraft had been lost in the attack itself, although most had been damaged by flak. And so, on 17 September 1944, the force took off for home. No bunting though. No banners. Certainly, no band. We were very markedly no longer Glorious Heroes to our Russian hosts!

There followed a short spell during which we mounted several army-support operations in Holland, the squadron delivering three softening-up attacks on the defences centred on the island of Walcheren.

We also attacked the Sorpe Dam, last raided on 17 May 1943 by No. 617 Squadron. For our raid, on 15 October 1944, No. 9 Squadron was given a free hand in planning the operation. To date, this was to be the deepest daylight penetration of the Reich by Bomber Command's main force and we were to be protected by nine squadrons of Mustang long-range fighters.

Our escort picked us up some fifty miles before the German border, after which we saw only the occasional burst of flak. Even our wind finding was less hazardous than normal, for once again the whole squadron flew the racetrack, with nobody being singled out. The need for accuracy had been stressed from the outset, and we rose to the occasion, one report calling this 'the most accurate piece of concentrated bombing ever accomplished'. Just the same, the Sorpe Dam was found to be proof against even the most accurately delivered Tallboys, after which it was tacitly accepted that it never had been a suitable target for air attack. Possibly it would have succumbed to the Grand Slam, the 22,000 pound successor to the Tallboy, employed later by No. 617 Squadron, but who knows.

As a squadron, the venture cost us nothing, but the always necessary blood price was paid by several Mustangs who fell prey to what flak there was.

And all too soon it was – bloody *Tirpitz* again!

We learnt that she had been taken south, to Tronso. Only this not only robbed her of sheltering cliffs but put her within range of our domestic airfields, although we still faced a 2,200 mile round trip. Offsetting that, no smokescreen had been laid on. So on 28 October 1944 we were *Tirpitz* bound once more.

The force made rendezvous over a singularly-shaped lake, after which our crew led the foremost wave of attackers to a point near enough to Tronso to determine a dropping-height wind. Our wind-finding duty accomplished, we raced flat out for the target, catching up just as the main force commenced its run-in, only to find *Tirpitz* totally concealed by cloud. Many other crews went around again but Pete dropped on the gun flashes once more, although with no great hope for the result.

As we droned home across the sea, with depression settling ever more heavily upon us, Mac first initiated, then, as we grudgingly joined in, led us, in an extempore and increasingly more obscene version of *The Ball at Kirriemuir*. And so we arrived back at our departure base of Lossiemouth after a thirteen-hour flight. On that occasion, I still feel, by relaxing his normally rigidly-enforced intercom discipline, Mac truly showed his stature as a captain.

Once again news merely trickled in. But all too soon we learnt that although some damage had been caused, *Tirpitz* remained an unacceptable threat.

On 11 November 1944, therefore, we set out yet again. My diary records, *Awaiting the signal to take-off I conjured up visions of the entire Luftwaffe waiting to pounce on us and prayed for a last-minute cancellation*.

Although Mac tried to keep us screened by the mountains, we had to climb above their shelter to get any meaningful wind. Only this brought a curtain of flak about us. But worse was to follow.

'Sorry, lads.' It was Pete. His bombsight had become unserviceable and he was calling for that most unwelcome of all manoeuvres, a go-around, necessarily to be followed by a second run-in through the flak. Mathematician Nigel, homerically, began recalling the sums that would enable him to carry out a manual drop, while Mac began the turn.

At least, the ensuing orbit afforded us a grandstand view of the bombing. We could track the Tallboys all the way down, but saw none score anything other than near hits – or near misses; though the pressure surge from either might well have been effective. A brief exchange of data between Nigel and Pete, then Pete called us in again and we held our breaths, not even daring to clear our throats in case we disturbed his concentration.

And suddenly, just as Pete announced, 'Bomb gone', and our lightened aircraft lurched upwards, so the flak died away. Our Tallboy exploded some twenty yards to port of the vessel. But already there had been a column of smoke. And now Geoff, in the rear turret, pealed out, 'Skip – *Skip! She's on fire*.'

As Mac banked over we all saw the blaze amidships, and then, an instant later, the emergence of the pinky-red colouring of her hull as *Tirpitz* began to roll. It was all we could have dreamt of!

After nearly thirteen hours in the air we once again touched down at Lossiemouth, tired beyond belief, but this time braced by the highest of high hopes. And sure enough, an indeterminate time later our sleep was disturbed as the gladsome tidings began to spread that *Tirpitz* had, in fact, turned turtle.

Celebrations followed, with congratulations from all over, from Winston Churchill downwards. Medals followed, scuds of them. Mac, Nigel and Pete, all three commissioned by now, got Distinguished Flying Crosses, as did pilots, navigators and bomb aimers on many other crews. Was it noteworthy, though, that in the whole force there were no decorations for flight engineers, wireless operators or air gunners, not even for those who had been on all three *Tirpitz* operations?

Anything after this could only be an anti-climax. Just the same, what did impress us were two night trips to Munich carried out on 26 November and 17 December 1944 respectively. These were so well planned and so well executed – the approach being made, rather naughtily, by overflying neutral Switzerland – that the defences did not respond until we had turned for home. What equally impressed us was the sight of night-time Switzerland, for since taking up flying none of us had ever seen a country lit up with peacetime illuminations.

The year turned, and in the early part of 1945 our tasks tended towards attacks on oil targets. One that comes to mind was the attack on the refinery at Leuna, near Leipzig, a nine-hour trip, six of which were over Germany, with its flak. Of course, as a crew, we had long since realised that Mac and Pete were often able to lose themselves in the job, especially during the run-up. The rest of us, though, were forced to sit and wait it out.

The next longish trip was to the Brux refineries at Prague, where the opposition was said to comprise a thousand anti-aircraft guns. And sure enough, as we ran in each and every one of them singled us out. Or so it felt. But once more we got away with it and turned for home unscathed, with awareness dawning as the Channel fell behind us that the end of our tour of thirty operations was looming. Suddenly, for the first time in ten months, we had a future!

We flew twice more. At which juncture Mac called a crew conference. What he put to us was that if we completed our tour we would be rested, but would then be summoned back six months later. Summoned back, as like as not, to fly with a new and probably untried bunch of chaps. The alternative was to apply to stay on as a special-duties crew, when just fifteen more ops would be reckoned as a full second tour. The proposal led to a lot of discussion, but finally, persuaded by his eloquence, we agreed to soldier on. And so we applied. And were accepted. And soldiered on.

In a sense this proved to be timely, for shortly after we had committed ourselves it was decided that the war situation had improved so much that first tours would now be thirty-five ops. It made no difference to us, of course, but it caused widespread concern to many crews whose only aim had been to finish their thirty and stand down.

Days later we set out to attack a railway viaduct near Kassell but were recalled due to deteriorating weather at Bardney. In the event we diverted to the emergency airfield at Woodbridge, in Suffolk, and Mac – now a flight lieutenant flight commander – carried out what the rest of us found to be a nail-biting blind approach with the aid of the petrol-burning, fog-dispersal aid known as FIDO (Fog Investigation and Dispersal Operation). And even then he pressed on below the laid-down limits! As we finally came to a halt a voice from the rear pleaded, 'Can we start breathing now?' Certainly it was the only time I kissed the grass on climbing down.

For a while after that we simply sped through our extra fifteen operations. And then, at the end of March 1945, things slowed right down for us. For a start, we were sent on leave. But even when we returned, things remained quiet

I particularly remember one occasion when an op was cancelled after we had boarded the aircraft. The squadron was formally stood down and, with nerves loosening, we rushed back to the Nissen hut to change and make off into Lincoln. Only for Mac to put a spanner in the works.

He wanted, he told us, to get airborne and practise a new corkscrew-evasion manoeuvre he had come across: it could be a life saver… Only we had finally discovered not just that he had a private agenda, but what it was: he wanted to continue flying after the war but still needed about a hundred more hours to qualify for his civil licence. Which accounted for all the extra training trips we had found ourselves doing!

I took it upon myself to object to flying during a squadron stand-down, at which he pulled rank, something he had never done before. And so, as all the other crews boarded the bus, we huffily reclaimed our parachutes and took to the air. We got over it. We were a crew. But for a day or two there was a definite atmosphere.

Another flight which struck me as equally unnecessary proved to be among the last of our operational trips. This was a long-range massed raid on Hitler's Eagle's Nest eyrie at Berchtesgaden, near Salzburg. As we sailed across Southern Germany enjoying the scenery there was no opposition whatsoever. We did our final wind-finding racetrack, and dropped our last Tallboy. But apart from gaining Mac another eight hours towards his civil licence it was a total waste of time. And thirteen days later the war in Europe ended.

One further trip we did was one of the official Cook's tours of Bomber Command targets for the groundcrew, overflying Cologne, Bremen, Essen, and Emden at just 2,000 feet and wondering at the destruction wrought. An unforgettable experience.

In stark contrast, our final jaunt came just after my twenty-first birthday, a noteworthy event which was twinned with an atomic bomb being dropped on Japan. Within days the war was over and the whole crew went absent without leave to celebrate in Piccadilly Circus. It was well worth it, although I was the only one actually charged with the offence, losing a day's pay, and some years later causing not a little head scratching among my commissioning board!

When VJ Day overtook us, we had been a crew for fifteen months. But even before that we had begun to break up. Jock had elected to remain with the squadron in its projected move to the Far East when, as part of Tiger Force, it was expected that it would press home attacks on Japan; while Pete was to transfer to the RAF Regiment. And within days Mac, Nigel and I, all of whom had expressed an interest in transport flying, were sent to Snaith, in Yorkshire, to the Transport Command Assessment Unit.

The shock outcome there was that Mac alone was refused, being told that his aircraft handling was too harsh! At the time, certainly, it seemed as if his career in civil flying was to be still-born but with his native-born cunning he duly engineered his way in and after that never looked back. And so, we went our separate ways.

Accepting demob in October 1946 I sat for the Civil Service examination and on the strength of having scored record marks, embarked upon a career in the police. In June 1947, however, by then unenamoured of my prospects as a bobby, I went through aircrew selection once again and found myself flying Dakotas, although Transport Command's practice of getting airborne without a parachute came as a shock to the system.

Posted to No. 114 Squadron at Kabrit in the Canal Zone, I settled to flying routes embracing a whole gazetteer of places around the Middle East and Africa.

In June 1949 we converted onto Vickers Valettas, getting to places a little more quickly but being plunged back into the days of steam wireless with the home-grown Marconi which, for all its coloured knobs, was far inferior to the Dakota's radio fit.

On returning home I was sent to No. 1 Air Signallers' School at Swanton Morley, in Norfolk, to instruct trainee Air Signallers. More significantly, I met and married Peggy. My next Service move, though, was to Swinderby, in Lincolnshire, to train re-entrants into the Service, many of whom had a hard time accepting that the peacetime RAF had far higher standards than those which had been obtained in wartime.

My instructional duties ended with a posting to Coastal Command where, by

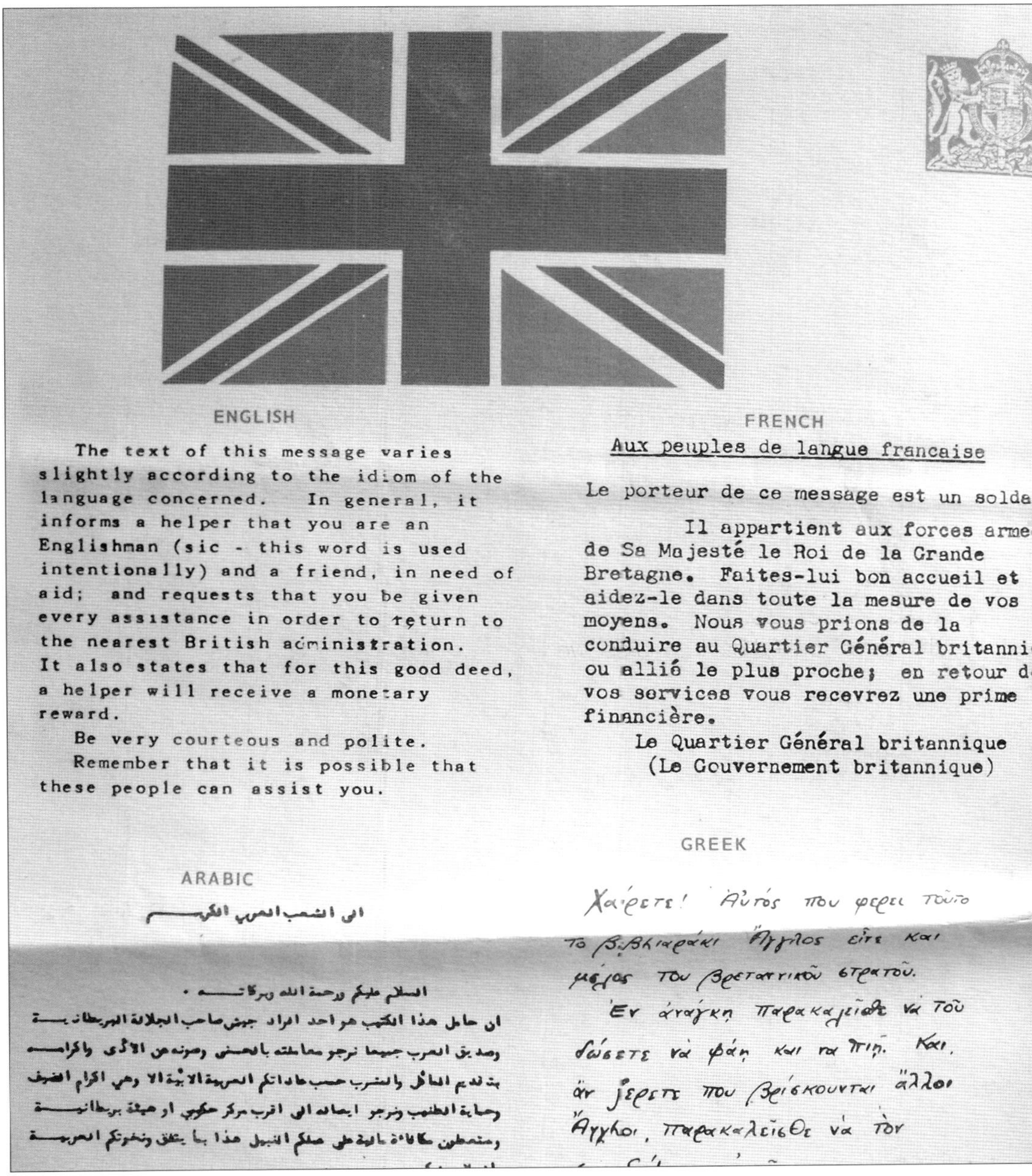

ENGLISH

The text of this message varies slightly according to the idiom of the language concerned. In general, it informs a helper that you are an Englishman (sic - this word is used intentionally) and a friend, in need of aid; and requests that you be given every assistance in order to return to the nearest British administration. It also states that for this good deed, a helper will receive a monetary reward.

Be very courteous and polite.

Remember that it is possible that these people can assist you.

FRENCH

Aux peuples de langue francaise

Le porteur de ce message est un solda

Il appartient aux forces arme de Sa Majesté le Roi de la Grande Bretagne. Faites-lui bon accueil et aidez-le dans toute la mesure de vos moyens. Nous vous prions de la conduire au Quartier Général britanni ou allié le plus proche; en retour d vos services vous recevrez une prime financière.

Le Quartier Général britannique
(Le Gouvernement britannique)

ARABIC

الى الشعب العربي الكريم

السلام عليكم ورحمة الله وبركاته .

ان حامل هذا الكتب هو احد افراد جيش صاحب الجلالة البريطانية
وصديق العرب جميعا نرجو معاملته بالحسنى وصونه من الأذى واكرامه
بتقديم المأكل والمشرب حسب عاداتكم العربية الابية الا وهي اكرام الضيف
وحماية الطنب ونرجو ايصاله الى اقرب مركز حكومي او هيئة بريطانية
وستمطون مكافأة مالية على عملكم النبيل هذا بما يتفق ونخوتكم العربية

GREEK

Χαίρετε! Αὐτός που φέρει τοῦτο
το βιβλιαράκι Ἄγγλος είτε και
μέλος του βρεταννικοῦ στρατοῦ.
Ἐν ἀνάγκῃ παρακαλεῖσθε νὰ τοῦ
δώσετε νὰ φάῃ και να πιῇ. Και,
ἂν ξέρετε που βρίσκουνται ἄλλοι
Ἄγγλοι, παρακαλεῖσθε νὰ τὸν

A goolie chit (Arabic).

Phil Tetlow in 2010.

applying myself and passing out at the top of the course I managed to secure one of the coveted places on Sunderland Flying Boats. To fly aboard such a luxury machine was an experience in itself. But my flying days were numbered.

In 1955, after thirteen years of flying, I lost my medical category and elected to remuster into Air Traffic Control. Then, in January 1961, I passed through the Officer Cadet Training Unit at Jurby, in the Isle of Man. After that I enjoyed an idyllic three years in Cyprus with Peggy, following on with a tour at the Lightning-equipped master diversion airfield at Wattisham.

At that juncture, though, as flight lieutenant with twenty-six years of service behind me, and the job-critical age of forty-five looming, family pressures dictated that enough was enough. In June 1968, therefore, I packed away my uniform for good.

In all I had flown nearly 3,000 hours. My forty-two bombing operations had taken 258 hours, with fifty-six of those being spent on our *Tirpitz* forays. Indeed, in the years since rejoining there had been yet more flying with an operational flavour when I had dropped supplies to starving Arabs in Yemen's Hadhramaut, dicing with a sun-baked dropping-zone set amid stark and threatening mountains that might well have doubled for a tide-lorn Norwegian fjord.

The terrain was hazardous enough, but although we carried 'goolie chits' – *x amount will be paid to the bearer when this airman is safely delivered to the British authorities* – we were warned that if we did come down the local women would have no mercy on us, regardless of the fact that we were dropping food to them.

So aircrew remained a magnet for women! But what a far cry from those heady days in Blackpool!

4

God, Honour, and Country

Warrant Officer Stanisław Józefiak, VM, KW and three bars
wireless operator/air gunner, later Spitfire pilot,
Polish Air Force under British Command

I was born in Skalmierzyce, Posnan, Western Poland, on 10 September 1919 and was bitten by the flying bug from my earliest days. When I was sixteen, therefore, I applied to the Air Force School at Bydgoszcz for pilot training. As it happened, their pilot quota was full, so I entered as a cadet wireless operator-cum-air gunner.

The first year of the three-year course covered educational and technical subjects and general military training. During the next two, cadets went their separate ways, the pilots to learn to fly while we others studied radio, not least the morse code, the requirement being to receive 100 letters a minute – or 'twenties', twenty words a minute, to the RAF, who reckoned morse speed by five-symbol groups. Alongside this we studied the theory of air gunnery. The only actual flying that came our way, however, was the occasional air-experience trip.

In the normal way of things our aerial gunnery practice would have been done when we joined our units. In 1939, however, with Germany becoming ever more threatening, our training was curtailed as the school made a precautionary move to Krosno, on the south-western border of Poland.

Not long after the move, at 0600 hours on 1 September 1939, I had just blown reveille – one of my cadet duties – when Dornier bombers appeared overhead and began bombing the airfield. They flew very low on that first, treacherous raid, carrying out one pass after another. Being fully kitted, and having run for the trenches I had helped dig just days before, I was able to let fly at them with my rifle. I don't think I scored a single hit, just the same I can claim to have taken the fight to the enemy from the very start of hostilities.

We soon found out that the Germans had launched a sudden invasion of Poland. Our trained airmen fought well, although it was later said that ninety-five per cent of

Cadets at the Polish Air Force School, 1938

those engaged in the short September Campaign died. Before doing so, however, they accounted for between 100 and 200 enemy machines.

Our ground forces too fought fiercely, but as they reeled eastwards so the school was evacuated by rail to Luck, in the north-east of Poland, near the Russian border. Then, on 10 September 1939, with the situation getting worse, we received orders to march south, in column, towards Romania.

The move was carried out by night to avoid air attacks. The route, though, took us through provinces annexed only a few years before from the Ukraine and now thronged with nationalist terror bands, obliging us to march at the alert.

As it was we crossed the bridge into Romania on 17 September 1939, the very day the Russians launched their totally unexpected onslaught from the east, their armies pincering our already hard-pressed forces against those of the Germans.

What we could not know was that the school's staff and instructors, following in the wake of our main column, were among the 8,000 Polish officers seized by the Russians during the September Campaign and murdered by them on 5 March 1940 – in a total of some 22,000 prisoners of status – in the *zbrodnia katyñska*, the Katyn Crime.

German aircrew shot down during the September Campaign.

From the outset, though vastly outnumbered, we Poles had taken strength from the assurance that our treaty-bound Allies, Britain and France, would spring to our aid. No such aid materialised, however. And though fighting gallantly to the last, on 6 October 1939, Poland was forced to capitulate.

More heartening, our government had made certain prearrangements for our withdrawal into then-neutral Romania. Nevertheless, we were forced to leave our transport and virtually all our equipment at the border post at Kuty.

Things were quite chaotic for a while but finally we heard that General Sikorsky had formed an army in France. Using a variety of wiles, a friend and I made our way to Bucharest, then to Constanza, on the Black Sea, sailing on the liners SS *Transylvania* to Beirut and the SS *Champolion* to Marseilles, where French army trucks were waiting to transport us to the Lyon-Bron airfield.

We arrived on 20 November 1939 but I was among those selected to finish our training in England, and finally ended that series of journeyings at RAF Eastchurch, on the Isle of Sheppey.

* * *

Polish airmen and air force recruits aboard a UK-bound transport ship, 1940.

'This is Lieut. Sienkiewics, Sir; we call him Smith to distinguish him from his friend Kryzyianowski, who's known as Jones.' 1944 Punch *cartoon by Hailstone.*

Learning English immediately became high on our agenda and although in May 1940, when we were moved to Blackpool, we found plenty of beautiful girls only too willing to help us improve, the language was to continue to pose a problem for our RAF counterparts.

More importantly, legislation was swiftly brought into being by which we became the Polish Air Force under British Command.

When France fell in June 1940 I was flying in Fairey Battles at the gunnery school at West Freugh, near Stranraer, qualifying as a sergeant air gunner. Then it was on to No. 12 Operational Training Unit (OTU) at RAF Benson, Oxfordshire, where I crewed-up with a pilot and navigator. Again we flew in Fairey Battles but also in wireless-equipped Avro Ansons, enabling me to round off my training as both gunner and wireless operator.

My next posting, in December 1940, was to No. 18 Wellington OTU at RAF Bramcote, in Warwickshire, after which, fully trained at last, I was assigned to No. 304 Squadron at RAF Syerston, Nottinghamshire. This all-Polish squadron became operational on 24 April 1941.

My crew, now swelled to six with the addition of a second pilot and two more gunners, comprised: Flight Lieutenant Bronisław Kuszczynski, pilot; Pilot Officer Jan Stanisław Woroczewski, second pilot; Flying Officer Cezary Wieczorek, navigator; Sergeant Józef Nilski, wireless operator/air gunner; me, Sergeant Stanisław Józefiak, wireless operator/air gunner; and Sergeant Józef Drodz, rear gunner.

My own first operation, a raid on Cologne, came in early May 1941 when I substituted for a flu-stricken rear gunner. Before being tasked for operations as a crew, however, we had to wait until the night of 27 May 1941 when we were sent to raid the heavily defended port of Boulogne, with me as the front gunner. The outbound flight was uneventful but having dropped our bombs and turned out to sea we were hit by anti-aircraft fire, the machine lurching into a spiral dive with one engine badly damaged. Initially Bron, our pilot, ordered us to bale out, but on regaining control he rescinded the order. Unfortunately, Józef Drodz in the rear turret, reacting instantly, had already jumped and having fallen into the Channel was never found.

I might have been equally quick off the mark myself, but on the Wellington not only were there two-leaf doors to the turret itself, but a bulkhead door to close off the fuselage which had to be operated by someone else, normally the navigator. I'd had no option, therefore, but to stay where I was.

Gradually losing height over the Channel, we finally crossed the English coast, only for the remaining, and by now sorely overworked, engine to catch fire just minutes later. Again Bron ordered us to abandon, although we were very low by the time he gave the order.

Earlier, Cezary, our navigator, had released me from the turret and, finding that the astrodome had been stowed in readiness for a possible ditching, I decided to use its

A Wellington, with its front turret on view – someone had to open the doors for you …

opening as an exit. Even then I got stuck and had to pull the ripcord to get the parachute to yank me free. But my luck held, for I missed the tailfin. Józef Nilski, who had been at the wireless operator's station, also got clear. Tragically my other three comrades, Bron, Jan and Cezary, crashed with the aircraft and died.

I landed in a tree, felt an agonising pain and realised that, among other things, I had broken my left leg. I seemed to hang there for an age but I was eventually taken in charge by the initially hostile – or certainly suspicious – Home Guard. I then had to undergo nine months of hospitals in Tunbridge Wells and RAF Halton, and convalescent centres in Blackpool and West Kirby, before I was able to return to the squadron. Józef Nilski, on the other hand, although physically uninjured, was so traumatised that he never flew again.

For me it was a long and wearying nine months. Not only nine months which put a temporary halt to the off-duty dancing I loved, but which saw me champing at the bit to get back to my comrades, for I knew that they were taking heavy losses.

By the time I was fit enough to resume flying – and dancing! – the squadron had moved from RAF Syerston to RAF Lindholme, in Yorkshire. Joining as odd-man-out meant that I had no crew. On the other hand the squadron welcomed a spare body, for there was always someone sick or recovering from wounds, on leave, or on a course, and because I could fly in three positions – as nose gunner, rear gunner or wireless operator – I was seldom off the flying programme. I also gained the most valuable of insights into the way other crews did things.

Of course, no crew liked having a stranger pushed upon them. Indeed, even when a known and respected flight commander decided to come along and see their operation there was always a certain stiffness, a formality that never normally existed. If a temporary crew member was to be accepted, therefore, it was necessary that a crew not only knew him and respected him but trusted him too.

As an all-Polish squadron in the relatively small 'Polish Air Force under British Command' we all knew each other, and if not personally, then certainly by repute. Reputation, therefore, counted for a lot. In my case they all knew that it had taken me nine months to get over my injuries but that I still wanted to fly. Then, when I notched up my thirty ops and refused to be rested but simply carried on, that was noted too.

People often ask those who flew about fear during operations. But few wartime fliers are in a position to give an informed opinion, the majority only having flown with their own crews. That was where my floating position served me so well, for I flew with dozens of crews in both Bomber and Coastal Commands and saw just how differently they went about things.

Most crews, I should say, did their best to faithfully carry out the task they were detailed to do: the losses were testimony to that. But at the end of the day each crew was its own master. Whether you decided to press home an attack against overwhelming opposition or whether, instead, you decided to turn off to a secondary target; whether you dropped your bombs where you thought the target was or whether, instead, you decided to brave the anti-aircraft fire and make another circle to make sure; such things were up to the crew concerned.

Crews, of course, tended to stick together, but I would see the very widest variations among them. Again, that was where trust would come in, for accepting me as they did they did not have to put on an act. I saw it as my duty to fit seamlessly into the space temporarily left in their number. What would have made my position untenable would have been to have them regard me as a spy. Still worse had I acted the spy and carried tales behind their back.

All such issues are basically moral ones, of course, which brings up the question of dropping bombs in the first place. For my part I had seen from day one how the Germans went about making war. Yet, strangely, I was never driven by revenge. Certainly, not consciously so. My viewpoint was always that I had been trained to do a job and that if I didn't do it then someone else – and probably another Pole far less qualified – would have to do it. As for bombing accuracy, well, we knew all about that. But then we were high in the sky and remote from the consequences. Not revenge, then. But the fact remained, as I had seen at Krosno, that the Germans started it. Our task was simple: to finish it.

Crews varied widely, however, in the way they went about the task. For instance, a standard method of operating was laid down. You climbed your Wellington to height, found the target, bombed it, or went to the secondary target if you couldn't bomb the primary. Then you turned for Britain, holding the height so that you remained well clear of anything but high-altitude anti-aircraft guns, searchlights and fighters. For my part, though, I preferred to fly with those pilots who, with bombs gone, would put the nose down and go for the ground, letting us fire at anything that took our fancy. It was against orders, for low down you were at the mercy of every sort of small-arms fire. We might argue, of course, that low flying only gave the defences a fleeting chance. The real motive though, was that shooting up the enemy at close hand was terrific fun and did a tremendous amount for morale!

In all, while flying as spare man, I was to observe my fellow squadron members during very nearly two tours of operations, through fourteen Bomber Command raids and thirty-nine Coastal Command patrols, fifty-three ops in total. And how I grew to admire them!

Of my Bomber Command operations most were to the Ruhr, to such targets as Hamm, Essen, Dortmund, Duisburg and Gelsenkirchen. But I also raided Lübeck, Borkum, Cologne, Bordeaux and St Nazaire. I remember such targets only too well.

Just the same, one raid stands out in particular, from March 1942. I was once again flying as front gunner in place of a sick man, when our aircraft was coned by searchlights as it penetrated one of the outer defence rings of Essen. Though the machine had suffered

Hamm railway junction, with bombs falling to the right of the photograph.

hits from anti-aircraft fire, my pilot for the occasion Sergeant Michal Omieliaszko, having taken what avoiding action he could, pressed on and completed the bombing run. On arrival at base, however, we found that we had been holed thirty times.

On the other hand, flying on another operation with that crew against heavily defended Dortmund we were unscathed.

Yet trauma was rarely far distant, not least on a night when I had been stood down. Just after midnight I ran to a Wellington which had crashed on returning from operations and burst into flames. It was a horrible experience. And one only slightly relieved when it was found that, against all the odds, the rear gunner had been tumbled clear of the inferno, surviving with minor injuries.

Between them the cadet college and the RAF had trained me to the highest standard as a wireless operator, but for most of the time on ops, being at the set meant not knowing what was going on outside. For my part, therefore, I far preferred to take up either the front or rear turret positions where I could see what was going on and where the guns gave me a fair chance of doing something useful should trouble occur.

It should be remembered that in those early days on the Wellingtons we were effectively flying alone. There might be a dozen aircraft from the squadron raiding the target but each one took off individually, navigated its own way out, dropped its bombs, then found its way home again.

We also had to consider the limitations of the Wellington itself. Getting coned by searchlights was a regular occurrence, for the Germans tracked us with sound locators, if not with radar. Later in the war the Halifaxes and Lancasters had performance enough to corkscrew, but not the Wellington. The best we could do, therefore, was hold the heading, accepting that any evasive weaving would simply slow us down and keep us within range of the defences for even longer.

In fact, there was an occasion over Essen when anti-aircraft fire took out one of our engines. Nevertheless, luck was with us. And on several counts. For a start, having just dropped our bombs, we were able to maintain a decent altitude. Then again we were flying a mark of Wellington which allowed us to turn the stopped propeller blades edge-on to the airflow; on one of our earlier aircraft the enormous drag of a windmilling propeller would certainly have brought us down. And, of course, we were lucky not to be hit again, or to be intercepted by fighters.

Then again, when we reached the English coast it was not one of those nights when fog had settled on our aerodrome, forcing us to land somewhere else. For this only too frequently happened with the British weather.

I have spoken of very human shortcomings in some crews; of a certain lack of discipline in others. But, as I have also said, the twelve bombing trips I flew after my return filled me with admiration for all the crews I accompanied. It was only too clear, however, that the last few months before my return had taxed the squadron grievously. The authorities had evidently come to the same conclusion for, in May 1942, No. 304 Squadron was taken off the Bomber Command battle order and formally transferred to Coastal Command's No. 19 Group.

The official line was that in view of the heavy losses the squadron was being rested. Rested! In fact we were to be employed in carrying out the maritime sweeps that were so vital to the British in keeping the Atlantic convoys running.

The task was to fly eight-hour, low-level, anti-submarine, anti-shipping sorties over the Western and South-Western Approaches and the Bay of Biscay; monotonous trips for the most part and not infrequently carried out in foul weather. At first we operated from RAF Tiree, in the southern Inner Hebrides, but shortly afterwards we moved to RAF Dale, in Pembrokeshire.

The most immediate difference in our new field of operations struck me at once. On bombing flights, fervently looking for clear weather over the target and untroubled runs out and back, we had only rarely found any of the three desirables. Now, on Coastal fighting patrols, we were seeking out trouble throughout every moment of the flight, only to despair, at times, of ever finding so much as a whiff of it.

They were monotonous flights indeed, but even more demanding, perhaps, because of that. For it took an immense amount of self-discipline to maintain a constant lookout when for hours, days, weeks, even months on end, there was nothing to see. Yet even leaving one's post to visit the toilet was fraught. For we all knew the way things happen. Just sixty seconds to run to the Elsan. And those are the very seconds in which the vital sighting is missed! At least a near-bursting bladder was an effective guard against dozing off.

For me, however, the monotony was spectacularly broken on the occasion, in early 1943, when I was acting as Flight Lieutenant Figura's front gunner. We had completed our patrol and were abeam St Nazaire when we crossed with a four-engined aircraft some way above us, heading landwards. None of us could positively identify it but it was almost certain to have been one of the German Focke-Wulf Condor long-range patrol aircraft. It was gone in a flash, so there was nothing we could do about it. But the sighting livened us up no end.

You can imagine my surprise then, when just minutes later, I saw a surfaced U-boat only two miles away, heading westwards away from St Nazaire and clearly setting out on a patrol. I wonder still that the skipper took me at my word without question. But everything went like clockwork, just as we had rehearsed it when carrying out drills.

I continued to direct the skipper until he and both the second pilot, Flight Lieutenant Lajba, and the navigator, Flight Lieutenant Kryszczuk, could see the U-boat for themselves. In the interim the navigator had passed our position to wireless operator Sergeant Krajewski who, in turn, had transmitted a priority warning signal to Group. The

Focke-Wulf Condor FW200C-4.

navigator, by far the busiest man aboard in this extremity, had then hurriedly descended into the bomb-aimer's position.

There were several reasons why a submarine would be on the surface. Possibly a fault. Possibly charging its batteries. Possibly pumping in fresh air. Or simply caught out by our unexpected appearance from the clouds. And this one really had been caught out, for it was nowhere near ready to dive.

Our skipper picked up his line, heading directly for the conning tower. The submarine didn't even get off a shot as we swept towards it. The bomb doors were open, the line-up was right, the speed was right, the height was right, everything was right. Just as per the book. The nav's finger clicked the switch. Only the depth-charges failed to release!

After all the hours and days and weeks of seeing nothing, for that to happen! But what it meant at the time was that suddenly we were in trouble. Unable to use our depth-charges, all we had as armament were our 0.303 calibre machine guns, mere pea-shooters compared with the heavy-calibre weapons the submarine mounted. Now our quarry of just moments before had all the time in the world to either submerge at its leisure or sit back and blow us out of the sky.

For our part we could do nothing but hold our heading until we got beyond range of its guns, leaving it to Sergeant Wanciszewicz, the rear gunner, to tell us what our adversary was doing. Meanwhile we sent an enhanced sighting signal and hoped that someone else with depth-charges that worked could get here in time, re-locate the U-boat and finish it off. It didn't happen, of course. And just moments later, at a call from the rear turret, the skipper banked over so that we all saw the submarine, tail high out of the water, doing an emergency eighty-degree dive before being lost to sight. Despite all the subsequent months of patrolling that was the only time I was to see such a thing! All we did get was a photograph. But no second chance.

What the U-boat crew thought about their miracle escape had to be a matter for speculation but there was a big inquiry when we got back. Though as everyone knew, weird technical things have a habit of happening in the air. At that time people used to speak of gremlins, little manikins whose job it was to cause such upsets as oil leaks, 'mag' drops – and hung-up depth-charges. And blaming it on gremlins is as close as the authorities came to determining what had gone wrong.

But we were a crew. And even though I was a spare man, I was part of that crew, trusting and trusted: as I have explained, having a spare man along would not have been tenable otherwise. So we were a crew. And we knew very well what had happened. We had not managed to work it out in time to set up another attack, but we had worked it out. Eventually. The navigator was the one who had the task of handling the switchery to release the depth-charges. And in his rushing about from station to station he had simply messed it up, operating the switches in the wrong order. It had been as straightforward as that.

And in war, just as in everyday life, events turn upon detail. In this instance had our nav only kept his finger out the Germans would have lost a submarine, who knows how many Allied mariners' lives would have been saved, and who can say just what extra volume of war cargo would have arrived safely in English ports. Most important of all: we would have been heroes! We knew what had happened, but the knowledge did nothing to console us.

Nor was morale improved when, on 12 August 1942, Sergeant Pilot Michal Omieliaszko and his crew, the men with whom I had survived the flak and searchlights over Essen, were killed when their aircraft plunged into the sea after a failed take-off from Dale.

The maritime patrols went on, but in March 1943 we were moved to RAF Docking, a satellite of Bircham Newton, in Norfolk, to carry out anti-E-boat patrols over the North Sea. And just months later, after I had flown some 400 hours on operations, firm directions were received from the Polish depot at Blackpool that Warrant Officer Józefiak – I had reached that exalted rank by then! – was to be compulsorily rested. The gods had spoken!

In the course of my fifty-three operational sorties I had become a four-times holder of the *Krzyz Waleczny*, the Cross of Valour. Now, my commanding officer smilingly told me to add the ribbon of the *Virtuti Militari*, Poland's highest military decoration. It was effectively a Victoria Cross equivalent, awarded, I was told, for my overall operational service.

Of more significance, as an extra reward it could be, I was given a choice of posting. I could either become an instructor, training other wireless operator/air gunners, or I could re-train as a pilot. In truth, I was not that sure what to make of the decoration but I knew how unusual it was for trained aircrew to be allowed to remuster to pilot during wartime. This rekindling of my childhood dream, therefore, posed no problem for me. The only decision to be made was whether to go on leave and join a course starting in three months' time, or give up leave and join a course starting right away. Need I say that I did not take the leave?

In July 1943, therefore, I was posted to No. 25 Elementary Flying Training School, at RAF Hucknall, Nottinghamshire. Initially though, this meant spending some months on ground-school studies at Brighton. Returning to Hucknall in December 1943 I finally started flying training. Gratifyingly, having wanted to fly as a pilot for so many years, I found that I took to it very well, going solo on a Tiger Moth in just seven hours and completing the initial course having logged sixty day and a few night hours.

My next move was to No. 16 Service Flying Training School at RAF Newton, near Nottingham, where, having been given the chance to opt for fighters or bombers, I chose fighters. This meant a transfer to the Miles Master advanced trainer which we flew at Tollerton, Newton's satellite airfield. Finally, in August 1944, with basic and advanced training completed, I received my pilot's wings, sporting the Polish insignia on my left breast and the RAF variant on my right.

I was then given a holding posting at RAF Cleave, near Bude, in

Spitfire 5B of No. 303 (Polish) Squadron.

Pilots of No. 317 Squadron at Ahlhorn, Germany.

Cornwall, where I flew single-engined Hawker Henley target tugs to exercise anti-aircraft units. This was followed by a ten week course at No. 61 (Fighter) Operational Training Unit at RAF Rednall, Shropshire, where I had another choice: to fly Spitfires or Mustangs. This was a hard choice, but eventually I chose the Spitfire.

Another holding posting followed, this time to RAF Lasham, in Hampshire. But in April 1945 I joined the Second Tactical Air Force, flying as an operational fighter pilot with No. 317 Squadron from what had recently been a Luftwaffe field at Quakenbrück, in Northern Germany. And on 8 May 1945 Germany capitulated. Just the same the squadron remained in occupation for another eighteen months, operating from Ahlhorn, near Oldenburg.

At the end of 1946 we returned to England, to RAF Hethel, Norfolk. But only a few weeks later I flew what for me, in some ways, was the saddest flight of the war. Of my life, indeed! Alongside other squadron comrades I flew to RAF High Ercall, Shropshire, where our Spitfires were to be scrapped. For me, after logging some 500 hours on the beauty, it was like saying goodbye to a much-loved steed.

Like all the Poles who had been fighting outside Poland, I now had a truly hard decision to make. Should I return to my family in now-communist Poland, or should I seek a life elsewhere, hoping by so doing that I could better assist Poland to regain her freedom? After much heart searching, I opted not to return.

Initially, I applied to stay on and fly in the RAF, knowing that some Poles had succeeded

Warrant Officer Józefiak (left) and compatriot await the farewell flight.

in doing that. But possibly all the vacancies had been filled and my application was not approved. So it was that I found myself posted to RAF Portreath, near Redruth, Cornwall, for enlistment into the Polish Resettlement Corps.

As a result of the selection procedures at Portreath I was sent to RAF Kinloss, in Scotland, for a two year period during which it was intended that I should augment my earlier knowledge of radio and electricity. In the event, I specialised in reconditioning generators. But the highlight of this stay in Scotland was meeting my wife-to-be, Margaret, at – where else but! – a station dance. An ex-sergeant in the ATS, Margaret had since trained as a hairdresser and was working in Forres. We married a year later after a largely cycle-borne courtship. And not long afterwards I travelled down to RAF Dunholme Lodge, in Lincolnshire, for demob.

Before I left the Air Force altogether, though, there was a touch of farce when I was down at Polish Headquarters in London tying up a few loose ends. Quite unexpectedly I was summoned to the office of a very high-ranking general. I protested that I was in civvies, but that made no difference, it seemed, and I was wheeled in just the same. The general was glowing, but evidently very puzzled.

'You have never collected your *Virtuti Militari*', he challenged. I have to say that it took me aback. The medal had been the very last thing on my mind. Indeed, I cannot say that it had ever been in my mind to that extent. 'How is that?' he pressed. I gathered my thoughts. And the first answer that came was the honest one. 'I suppose I've been too busy, Sir,' I told him.

That really tickled him. And although I was no longer truly in the Service he made a solemn ceremony of the presentation. At the time I was more than a little bemused. But perhaps the significance of the honour my country had paid me took some time to sink in.

I now had to find a new way of life. Ascertaining that jobs in textiles were available in Derby, Margaret and I moved there, eventually buying a house which we named Kinloss after the RAF station where we had met. In fact, opportunities arose to fly for both the Pakistan and Argentinian air forces but I decided that the time had come to settle, and turned them down.

After a while I found a job at the Derby-based British Celanese Company, first as a fireman, then in the testing laboratory, but I have to say that neither of these extended me. At about that time, however, I was approached by a former air force friend who told me that, if I was interested, he could put me in the way of some profitable flying. I was both interested and intrigued, and urged him to press my case with the shadowy prospective employers whom he would not name.

Even now I cannot say all that much about the details of the business except that these employers were the American Central Intelligence Agency. Nor was joining them something to be hastily arranged, for after several interviews I had to wait nearly a year before being called forward. The moment the call came, however, I gave in my notice at Celanese.

What I can reveal is that our operating base was in Greece, not that far from Athens, and our work, clandestine insertion operations throughout the Balkans and Southern Europe. There were several such CIA units operating but ours was wholly Polish. For that reason we adopted false names; even letters written home were addressed to an office, then re-dispatched.

Again, regarding the aircraft, I shall only say that they were of the Boston-cum-Mitchell variety, twin-engined, dependable, and modified to be capable of dropping people by parachute. People, and very occasionally, packages. Among the five or six CIA crew members, my role was that of wireless operator.

The night flying was rather different from that I had experienced during wartime years, for now every town and tiny settlement was lit up. Our dropping zones, though, were always in remote areas and not infrequently sited in difficult, and even mountainous, terrain. On occasion the receiving party might have a radio beacon on the style of the old wartime Eureka homer, but more often we would have to mapread our way and locate the dropping zone by visual signals and ground panels. Although our first priority, having sighted the dropping zone, and certainly before dropping our agents, was to double-check its authenticity and so confirm that it was not a decoy set up by the opposition. For the main thing these operations shared with my wartime flying was the presence of people only too willing to shoot at us from the ground. They even hit us on occasion, but our method of flying very low and with no pre-declared route meant that they had to be very lucky if they were to inflict enough damage to bring us down.

There were Soviet-bloc – Warsaw Pact – fighters on the prowl, but although we tended to fly on moonlit nights, the terrain hid us from their controlling radars. Unlike the unfortunate Gary Powers in his U2 spy plane, we were not up against anti-aircraft missiles. But if he, when asked how high he had been flying, habitually answered, 'Not high enough', we – should anyone have asked – could have replied, 'Just low enough, thank you.'

It was fascinating flying, exciting and utterly unlike the drudging toil at British Celanese. Additionally, it paid infinitely better; indeed I would make in one month what it had taken me six months to earn at Celanese. Even better, working for the CIA meant that living was pretty nearly all found! Better times still came in the second year of my contract, when Margaret and our baby son, Robert, were allowed to join me.

All in all, Margaret loved the eighteen months she spent out there, for Greece really is a wonderful country. Indeed, I think, on balance, the climate and the off-duty lifestyle – not forgetting the inflated salary! – suited us so well that we might have stayed in Greece indefinitely. Only then the British spies, Burgess and Maclean, put a spanner in the works.

Around that time there was a tremendous amount of political intriguing, with everyone in the West mincing around on tiptoes for fear of upsetting precious Russia. As it happened, I had just become a naturalised Briton. Next thing I knew the British had put the screws on the Americans declaring that they couldn't accept their subjects being recruited as we had been. We had an option, which was to accept American naturalisation and carry on in the job. But after Margaret and I had discussed it we decided that enough was enough, and we gave way gracefully and resumed our life in Derby.

Stanisław Józefiak in 2010.

For a time I returned to work for others, but as a side venture we opened a shop selling furniture and carpets which eventually became so successful that it demanded our full-time attention.

Meanwhile the political climate in Poland had begun to change, so that in 1961 I was able to begin visiting my homeland for the first time in twenty-two years. Even then the visits proved fraught, with a requirement to report daily to the police. Indeed, that first visit was extremely unsettling, for the police presence was very obvious. But conditions gradually improved so that in June 1992 I was a guest-participant at the 200th anniversary of the *Virtuti Militari* award.

Long before that I had become standard bearer and chairman of the Derby branch of the Polish Air Force Association in Britain. Time, though, took its toll among our members and in the end a decision had to be made about closing down the branch and laying up the standard.

A dispute arose with the curators of the Sikorski Museum in London who considered themselves to be the proper custodians. The dispute grew acrimonious when I objected, arguing that a standard laid up in a museum would simply gather dust; that its proper resting place was with the Polish Air Force in Poland. Finally, as the standard had been bought and paid for by the Derby Branch, I carried the day, just as I had, indeed, the standard. In particular, the museum held that nobody in Poland would value the standard. How wrong they were! The Polish Air Force were delighted to receive it and have held it in veneration ever since. Indeed, it was subsequently joined by the standard of the London Branch, no doubt to the dismay of the doubly-disappointed museum!

The Derby standard presentation had brought me into contact with the many senior officers of the Polish Air Force who had welcomed the continuity that the standard, and former airmen like me, represented. Following that initial meeting these contacts were cemented over the years during various official functions. Additionally, in the course of this renewed association with the domestic branch of the service I had left, effectively, in September 1939, I was promoted to the rank of major.

But I treasure other associations too, equally old. Indeed sixty-six years had rolled by when, in May 2000, I made the long-delayed, but equally long considered, pilgrimage to where my crew had died returning from our first op. I discovered that although I had landed at Hatfield, near Tunbridge Wells – the farmer was even able to show me the tree I had fallen into! – the plane had come down at Netherfield (Darwell Hole), in Sussex. And it was there, during 2000 and 2001, that I raised a memorial to them. This, I felt, was truly fitting, although all three, in fact, still lie at peace in the Polish Air Force cemetery at Newark.

Back in 1946 an article in *The Times* held that, soldiers aside, 2,500 Polish airmen were killed during the war; that nearly 70,000 additional Poles left Russia in 1942, and 12,000 more made their way to the UK from the continent during the conflict, each determined to continue to fight for the honour and freedom of Poland.

5

'It's a DFM for you...'

Flight Sergeant Syd Richardson
flight engineer

I was brought up in Birch Vale, between Hayfield and New Mills, in Derbyshire, and for as long as I remember had wanted to fly. In 1941, therefore, when I became eligible I applied to join the RAF as a pilot. My application was refused outright, however, for being an apprentice engineer I was in a reserved occupation. As it happened, the Air Training Corps had started by then, so as it seemed be the closest I could get to flying I joined, steadily rising to flight sergeant. Just a year or so later, though, at the beginning of 1942, I saw a newspaper announcement saying that many men in reserved occupations could now either fly in the RAF or serve in submarines: as you can imagine, there were no options as far as I was concerned!

So it was mid-1942 before I managed to have my application for aircrew accepted. I went to Padgate, near Warrington, for three days of medicals and aptitude tests and was assessed as suitable for pilot, navigator or bomb aimer, the top three in the aircrew hierarchy; after that came wireless operator, flight engineer and air gunner. However, when I was actually called up and returned to Padgate I was asked if I would remuster to flight engineer. I had to be asked, it should be understood, for aircrew were all volunteers. The request did not come as any great surprise to me, for at that period the RAF's priority was heavy bombers and they were desperate for flight engineers to man them, hence the relaxation in the reserved occupation rules, and, of course, I had an engineering background.

Having agreed to make the switch, I did a nine months' course at St Athan, starting off learning about basic aircraft systems then concentrating on those built into the Lancaster. There was no flying involved, but believe me, the school's equipment was so good that they were well able to do all the training on the ground. So much so that at the end of the course, when I was promoted to sergeant and was able to sew my FE (Flight Engineer's) brevet on my left chest, my feet still hadn't left the ground! Not that I admitted this to anybody during my course-end leave.

Regarding the brevet, a little later they dropped the 'F' so that future engineers wore a lone 'E'; but not for us oldsters: our FEs were firmly sewn on, and stayed there until they – or we – wore out!

My next posting was to Boston Park, Doncaster, an aircrew reception – or crewing-up – centre. Here we were issued with our flying gear and allocated to the type of aircraft we were to fly. I wanted to go onto Sunderland Flying Boats but allocations were done alphabetically. My name began with R, which, it seemed, meant Lancasters. In the same way others went onto Stirlings, Liberators, and Halifaxes. One of my friends actually went to Sunderlands and I was particularly jealous of him for I wanted to travel abroad, like he did. Of course, in the event, I did. Except that while I did plenty of continental journeyings – forty-five reckonable operations, and a couple more besides – I invariably came back to this country early the next morning!

Regarding forming crews, by 1943 – at Doncaster, at any rate – there was no question of crews being put in a room and mutually selecting themselves; your name simply appeared on a typed list headed by a pilot's name, and that was that. On the other hand, this method of allocating individuals to a crew removed the fear which mutual selection brought with it – confessed to by many men I met later – of not being chosen, and of being left like a wallflower on the side of the dance floor.

Of course, it might well have been that the crew I found myself allocated to had, in fact, originally come together by the mutual-selection method, for the five of them had been flying on the Wellington Operational Training Unit and had even carried out an operational sortie.

Having me and the mid-upper gunner join them swelled their number to seven: Sergeant Kenneth Patrick (Pat) Cochrane Doyle, pilot (later Flight Lieutenant, DFC); Sergeant Dave Winlow, navigator; Sergeant Fred Astle, bomb aimer (later Pilot Officer, DFC); me, Sergeant Syd Richardson, flight engineer; Sergeant Doug Green, wireless operator/air gunner; Sergeant Eric Fletcher, mid-upper gunner; and Flight Sergeant Geoffrey Charles Chapman-Smith, rear gunner, Royal Australian Air Force (later Pilot Officer, CGM – Conspicuous Gallantry Medal).

Before getting down to final training with my crew, however, I went up to Stockport on a maker's course, between lecture sessions paying frequent visits to the factory to see the various stages of construction the Lancaster went through. The course completed, I rejoined the others at Faldingworth, Lincolnshire, at No. 1667 Heavy Conversion Unit, where – to my dismay, a dismay bordering on disgust – we spent about a fortnight on the Halifax. I'd trained on the Lancaster systems, seen the machine take shape in the factory, only to have the Halifax thrust upon me at Faldingworth! Typical RAF! Thrown in at the deep end with a vengeance. True, both aircraft had Merlin engines but all the systems were different. Just the same, we muddled through.

Trainee crews were not allocated an aircraft of their own so we tried to avoid being detailed to fly the older machines. This was because the original Halifax tail units with angled leading edges to the fins had given trouble: essentially, they could be fatally stalled. However, once the fins had been changed to a rectilinear, straight-edged shape – like a playing card long way up – the problem disappeared.

As it was, with No. 300 (Polish) Squadron sharing the station and doing all the OTU's servicing, we had little enough choice, merely taking any aircraft that was available. Then, at the end of the course we were posted to Kelstern, Lincolnshire, and allocated to the embryo No. 625 Squadron.

Kelstern was a satellite of Binbrook, near Louth, where No. 625 Squadron was to form with Lancasters. The first few crews actually moved in during October 1943 but the airfield was far from finished when we arrived. Accommodation was primitive and there were Irish labourers everywhere. On the plus side there was not a Halifax to be seen.

Certainly, I was much happier once we got onto the Lancaster. Regarding the crew stations, mine was to the right-rear of Pat, my pilot. Much of the time I stood at his shoulder but I had a collapsible seat which could be swivelled and dropped when I needed to manage the fuel systems. My actual instrument panel was on the right-hand side of the cockpit but the gauges for all the engines shared the main instrument panel with Pat's flight dials.

As an outline of my on-board duties, once all the pre-flight checks were completed and all four engines running, Pat and I would do a mag-drop check on each of them – mag, for magneto, or ignition – and ensure that the ignition circuits were functioning within limits. After that, on the actual take-off, he would move the throttles to the gate, then put both hands on the wheel, leaving me to take the levers up to full power.

During flight I'd do all the fuel balancing and monitor the various panels for a whole host of parameters, retaking each reading every twenty minutes: temperature, pressure, boost and revs, fuel consumption, gallons gone and rate of flow, also flap pneumatic pressure. Indeed, I found an additional duty on one flight when we were coned by our own searchlights over Newcastle. The flight engineer's position had a downward identification light so I keyed in our aircraft letter in morse, and the searchlights immediately went out. Unfortunately it wasn't to work that way over Germany.

Finally, on landing, I would again position myself behind Pat. He would call for the flaps, which I'd then set, although he'd normally do his own throttles, knowing just the same that I was poised to give a hand if necessary.

As a pilot, Pat had a Sutton safety harness, combining shoulder and lower-body restraint, but I only had a lap strap. It was understood, therefore, that if it came to a crash landing he would send me to the rear, otherwise I'd have risked being catapulted out. That was the plan, anyway!

Dave Winlow, our navigator, sat to our rear busying himself with his H2S [map-display

A Lancaster pilot and his flight engineer liaise before take-off.

radar], Gee box [navigational radar], charts, his plotting table and his other bits and pieces of esoteric wizardry. Indeed, he never moved. Except for the occasion, very early on in our tour, when we were over Berlin and Pat called him forward to have a look. Dave came up. Craned out. Took in the bomb-bursts and flames, the cascading markers, the flak, the tracers looping upwards, the fingering searchlights, the shapes of other Lancasters, some so close... 'Jesus Christ!' he muttered, and went back to his cubby hole. After which we never saw him again during ops. 'I've got my curtain closed,' he'd tell us if we suggested he came forward again, 'and that's the way it's staying.' Nor, from what I heard, was he the only nav to do his tour-and-a-half like that.

Further back was Fred Astle, the bomb aimer, who would come forward when he needed to, both to aim the bombs and to man the front turret. Behind him was the wireless operator, Doug Green. Then came Eric Fletcher, the mid-upper – his turret being mid-way back along the fuselage, beyond the double main spars – and finally, Smithy, our colonial, way back in the rear turret. Rear-end-charlies, we called his breed, sometimes rear gunners, but never tail gunners: that was the American term.

On the Lanc there was no second pilot and although flight engineers were shown how to fly straight and level in the Link trainer we had no formal flying training. On one memorable occasion, however, I was filling a space for another crew whose bomb aimer, a Canadian by the name of Jack Chislet, was a washed-out trainee pilot. It seemed he'd been harping on about flying the aircraft. So when the pilot had to go back to the Elsan toilet and handed over to me, Jack pressed, 'Hey, Skipper, you promised next time would be my go.'

And so the skipper okayed it, and went off down the back. Jack clambered into the seat but in doing so put his boot on the flap lever. I reversed the control at once, but still the aircraft reared nose high! An instant later the skipper was with us again, although how he managed to get into the seat with his trousers around his ankles I could never work out. After which I'm told the would-be pilot never expressed the least interest to have another go. Nice to know, though, that, having left the squadron, he was decorated and eventually became a wing commander. And good luck to him, for flying with another crew never felt quite right.

16 December 1943: 'Black Thursday' they called it, not least because the weather was so foggy, cutting down even what little light there was. Just the same the overall weather pattern was such that we had to abort the night's op because of the heavy thunderstorms on the way to the target. There was St Elmo's Fire, and such a build-up of ice that the engines began surging so markedly that we couldn't maintain height despite jettisoning our bombs in the North Sea. In fact, Pat had actually given the order to bale out when we came over the Wolds, saw the ground and were able to put down at Ludford Magna.

A month later it was my twenty-first birthday, 29 December 1943, a fateful day which I celebrated with a trip to Berlin. We were overhead the city at 19,000 feet and had just let go our bombs. As always the lightened aircraft began to rise, when suddenly there was a violent shaking. Then a vibration started, some of which seemed to come from one of the engines.

Pat gave the preparatory order, 'Prepare to abandon aircraft.'

'I'll go back and have a look-see, Skipper,' I said.

'Before you go, Ricky,' he said, keeping his voice low despite the racket, 'have a look at this.' He seemed to pull at the wheel, then push at it. Only nothing happened! We simply continued in a gentle climb. But it was clear that we had lost our elevator control – nose up and nose down. Whether the elevator trim was still working and giving him some measure of control, I never did discover. I scrambled to the rear, squeezing past the others hastily preparing for the anticipated order to jump.

Four-pound hexagonal, thermite stick-incendiaries spilling from clusters.

Having negotiated the two main spars it was to find the fuselage awash with incendiaries! Clearly a Lancaster directly above us had let go its load and some of the incendiary element had come through our cabin roof! *Some of them*? Eighteen of the buggers! These were not the twenty pounders, thank goodness! but the four-pounder hexagonal stick variety that would have been spilled from a four-pack cluster of 240 or so, each bomb being some twenty inches long by one and a half thick.

Others must have caused the engine damage. Fortunately, none of them had ignited. But it might only be a question of time. Telling myself that the gently climbing aircraft was

A flare chute (left) *and stowed flares.*

not likely to fall out of the sky in the next moment or two I rushed about, and managed to jettison all eighteen of them down the flare chute.

After that I was able to turn to the elevator problem. The reason for this was equally self-evident, for of the two aluminium control rods running down the port side of the fuselage, one had been severed by a falling bomb!

After a moment I decided I'd best try to splice the broken rod. On the squadron we'd been supplied with a canvas toolbag, not that I'd even unzipped it before. But inside I found a small hammer, a large screwdriver, an adjustable wrench, a set of box spanners; that sort of thing. No wire, though, or adhesive tape. But the spare headset stowed by the rear turret had quite a lengthy electrical lead. Cutting this off, then butting together the fractured rod-ends, I wound the lead around the joint, using the screwdriver as a windlass to tighten the splice as much as possible. On the intercom, in order not to unduly alarm anyone else, I merely told Pat, 'Try it.' And watched.

The splice held when he pulled back on the wheel. When he tried pushing nose down, however, it came apart! Hurriedly now, suddenly all fingers and thumbs, I started work afresh. And this time it seemed to hold! 'OK,' I told him then. But, scrambling back to his shoulder and leaning close, I advised, 'It won't hold if you throw it around. So handle it easy. And steer clear of bloody fighters.'

On the strength of this partial success, Pat cancelled the order to prepare to abandon. And fortunately any enemy fighters steered clear. So handle it easy he did, treating the stick – the wheel – like eggs the whole way back. As just the two of us knew about the state of things with the controls the rest of the crew weren't quite as put out as we were when we arrived at the emergency landing airfield at Woodbridge, in Suffolk, and Pat had to go around again. As you'll appreciate, we were both more than glad after the second approach to feel the undercart hit the ground.

Next morning, back at Kelstern, the flight commander shook my hand. 'It's a DFM for you, Ricky,' he assured me.

Very gratifying. Only a few days later we were posted, and that was the last I heard of it. So, no medal, although some months later I was given a mention in despatches. But then, with even the most normal of ops, all any of us were ever really interested in was being down safe and well once more.

The new posting, on 1 January 1944, was to No. 7 Squadron, Pathfinder Force (PFF) at RAF Oakington, for although we had completed just eight ops we'd been offered the chance of transferring to this elite force and had accepted. As it turned out we had barely settled at Oakington when another PFF unit, No. 156 Squadron, suffered particularly heavily on a Berlin raid and we were reassigned to them, the transfer occasioning a move to Warboys, near Chatteris, in Huntingdonshire.

Of all the ops I did from Warboys – indeed, from anywhere – that one on the night of 15 February 1944 has to loom largest. It was to be our eighth visit to Berlin, except that as we approached the target we were singled out for a joint attack by a Focke-Wulf Fw190 and a Messerschmitt BF110. They liaised very cleverly, the Messerschmitt wing waggling and flashing its navigation lights but initially remaining just outside the effective range of our guns, the Focke-Wulf closing surreptitiously and letting us have it. The attack coincided with a call from Smithy that the Messerschmitt had exploded. By that time, however, we knew we were in trouble ourselves.

The aircraft had been raked along its length, the tailwheel had been shot off, while the hydraulics were so badly damaged that the bomb doors would not open and the flaps were left dangling. The rear turret suffered as did the mid-upper turret, but of immediate concern the propeller of the port outer had been hit, setting up such a severe vibration that Pat had great difficulty in maintaining control as, cursing, he turned for home. Just minutes from the target, but with our bombs trapped on board! At a nod from him I stopped the damaged engine and feathered the prop. Then, seeing that Pat had regained at least some measure of control, I made my way to the rear.

Doug Green, our wireless operator, who had seconds before reported flames from the back end, came aft with me, to find gunner Eric Fletcher lying on the floor beneath the mid-upper turret, moaning in pain. One of the bursts had caught him and then, wounded as he was, he had dropped from the turret and broken his leg! Doug busied himself getting Eric forward over the spars to the rest position where he could be given a shot of morphine while I continued rearwards.

Arriving at the rear turret, and peering through the clouds of smoke billowing from what turned out to be Smithy's burning parachute, I found an awful mess. Having beaten out the flames with my gloves I turned to the turret, to find that its doors had been so seriously damaged that they could only just be opened. When I tried to extricate Smithy, however, he would have none of it. 'Just leave me alone,' he insisted, 'as Eric's out of action I'm needed here.'

He was adamant. And so I had to leave him there, obviously badly wounded and in pain but determined to stick to his shot-shattered, freezing-cold post. And indeed, the Focke-Wulf did make another attack, but meeting determined resistance, fired low, passed beneath us and disappeared for good.

Making my way forward again I discovered that the gale whistling through the holes in the aircraft had made a shambles of the navigator's station. Dave's charts and logs had gone heaven only knew where. Not surprisingly, having to work under these conditions upset his calculations, so that some while later we strayed over Texel, in the Frisian Islands, and came under heavy fire, one shell hitting the throttle box and causing the starboard inner to run so wild that Pat had to start in all over again to maintain control.

Eventually, though, things settled down, and I was able to get to work on releasing the hydraulic pressure on the bomb-door jacks. The moment we reached the Channel, therefore, we were able to let the bombs go, dropping them onto the closed doors and trusting that their weight would force them open. As it did, but for one five-hundred pounder, which we were forced to carry back with us. It was the second time we had been forced to let our load go over the sea!

And only now, when we were well clear of the enemy coast, did Smithy allow us to set about releasing him from his turret. It took some doing, indeed by the time Fred Astle, Doug Green and I, spelling each other with the fire axe, had broken down the doors, then got him forwards, Dave had already brought us to a landfall that enabled Pat to set up for an approach at the same long, wide, emergency landing airfield we had used before, at Woodbridge.

It was clear that the landing would be fraught but there was no question of baling out with two seriously wounded men on board, more especially as the fire had reduced Smithy's parachute to a smouldering mess. So, a crash landing it had to be. The rest of the crew put their backs to the main spar, Fred and Doug supporting Smithy and Eric. For my part I took station beside Pat, ready to assist him in any way I could.

Flight Sergeant Geoffrey Charles Chapman-Smith, CGM, crew and family members at the Buckingham Palace investiture.

He made one approach but wasn't satisfied and so went around again to get a better line-up. With no wheels he was forced to touch down on the bomb-bay doors, which he duly did, if with something of a bump. As I have said, Pat had a full Sutton harness restraining him, but as for me, having no chance to move aft as the theoretical drill called for, I had to brace my boots against the instrument panel. Even so I was propelled forwards and got a bang on the head which knocked the senses out of me.

The saving grace was that there was no fire. Just the same the aircraft was in such a state that the rescue crew decided that the best way to remove our casualties was to chop through the fuselage.

Eric, the mid-upper gunner survived, and mended well. Smithy also survived. However, he had to lose his leg. On the plus side the surgeon told us that had we moved him from the freezing-cold turret into the relative warmth of the fuselage any earlier he would certainly have bled to death. It may have been some consolation to Smithy (Flight Sergeant Geoffrey Charles Chapman-Smith) that he received the Conspicuous Gallantry Medal (CGM) for his courage. A rare distinction indeed, with only a hundred and three CGMs awarded during the Second World War as opposed to some 7,000 DFMs and 21,000 DFCs! The Aussie's only comment, however, was, 'If it hadn't been for the Skipper we'd none of us have got back.'

Having seen things tidied up inside the aircraft I joined the rest outside. I must have been looking as rocky as I felt after that bang on the head, for an airman moved in to steady me.

"Where're you from?" he asked, clearly meaning either the target or our home station.

'From Birch Vale,' I told him woollily.

'Small world,' he grinned, 'I'm from Glossop.' That is, from the town just a few miles up the road from my home!

The core of the crew was soon back on ops, flying as before from Warboys. In March 1944, however, progressing in seniority as a pathfinder crew as loss followed loss, we moved to Upwood, a change of scene that almost immediately gave me lots to think about. I'd just come back from an op and was getting my head down when a Mosquito landed, swung off the runway and careered into our billet. The aircraft went up, and the hut with it. I was hospitalised, and left with nothing but my pyjamas, my Irving jacket and the silk, polka-dot scarf I always used to fly in. Everything else went. But in other respects I had come out of it better than could have been expected.

It was a few days before I was fit again. In the interim, Pat Doyle, my pilot, had finished his second tour, sixty hard ops during a period when no ops were easy. By now he was a flight lieutenant and had gained a DFC. Bomb-aimer Fred Astle, though, now a pilot officer, DFC, had another op to do. So, on 24 September 1944, Pat went along

Syd Richardson in 2008

to keep him company. It was only to Calais. And 'only' was the way we thought of Calais at that time – in common with many French targets – a mere milk run. Just the same, they were shot down over the target, neither surviving.

Returning to flying duties, I soldiered on, but after I had flown eight operations of my second tour – thirty-eight in total, for the aborted sorties didn't count – the war in Europe came to an end.

Not that the war had ended for us, it seemed, for our squadron was among those selected to form part of Tiger Force, the Very Long Range (VLF) Bomber Force which was to be based in Okinawa to support the invasion of Japan. In preparation for this our Lancasters were repainted with black undersides and white upper surfaces, and there was at least a provisional move to fit the in-flight refuelling equipment that the lengthy return-legs of the Pacific Theatre would call for. Then the atomic bombs were dropped, Japan surrendered, and it really was all over. Not for the first time, we counted ourselves lucky.

As things wound down I was posted to RAF Leeming, in Yorkshire, where my luck continued to improve. At a dance in the Brompton-on-Swale village hall I met Willina. Her mother hated hackneyed names and had adapted the quality of being 'Willing' to serve her daughter as a first name, although it has long become Lyn. A year later we married, and by 2008 had enjoyed sixty-two years of married happiness.

As my marriage started, though, so my flying career came to a halt. For me, it was the end of an era. But high time for a rest, I suppose.

But Willina – Lyn – admitted to no mere supposition. 'For years afterwards,' she recalled, 'he would have these dreadful nightmares, reliving it all over again in his mind.'

There is a coda to the above. For Syd regularly attended the No. 156 Squadron reunions. Then, after two years' absence due to illness, he told a friend that he did not feel up to going any more. The friend, who piloted an AWACS (Airborne Warning and Control System) E-3 Sentry aircraft as a day job, also flew the Battle of Britain Memorial Flight's Lancaster. On a Saturday afternoon in May 2008, therefore, a Lancaster appeared and commenced a series of low passes over Syd's house. An emotive enough sight for anyone. And for the person to whom the tribute was paid?

'Tears filled my eyes,' Syd confessed. 'I couldn't keep them back.'

6

One of the Few

Flight Lieutenant Albert Edward Gregory, DFC, AE
wireless operator/air gunner

It always leads to raised eyebrows when, as a former wireless operator/air gunner, I am introduced as 'one of The Few', but although the Hurricane and Spitfire boys played the major part in the Battle of Britain, we aircrew lads were in the fray too. As it was, I was destined to fly on after the Battle and indeed throughout – and even after – the war, successfully evading the clutches of Bomber Command and its heavies and flying as crew on light-bomber types. Great years! Years, for me, that started when, in April 1939, I joined the Royal Air Force Volunteer Reserve (RAFVR).

I was born in Derby on 9 May 1917 and having left school joined the Co-op in its horse-and-cart transport division. After the Munich crisis in 1938 it was evident that a war was brewing, so when I applied to the RAFVR I was accepted as a trainee wireless operator/air gunner. The Derby 'Town Centre' Training Establishment, where I began my training – and rose to become a leading aircraftman – was located at Highfields, on the then outskirts of the town, in fact, just behind the Broadway pub on the A6, although only the main gates now remain.

The VR was mobilised on 1 September 1939, just two days before war broke out, and within a matter of weeks I was among a group posted to Aldergrove, in Northern Ireland, to undergo training as an air gunner. In December 1939, having completed the course, I joined the strength of No. 141 Squadron at Grangemouth, Scotland. As it transpired, this was to be the only *non-operational* squadron time I was to do throughout my service!

Until April 1940 we flew Blenheim bombers but then converted to the Defiant fighter. I found my six-foot one inch height no bar to operating the Defiant's rotating dorsal – that is, back-mounted – turret, even wearing the combined parachute and flying suit especially designed for Defiant crew members. However, a ruling came in that five-foot ten was the limiting height for Defiant gunners, so I was posted to the newly-reformed No. 219 Squadron at Catterick, in Yorkshire.

A short-nosed Blenheim Mk.1.

No. 219, I found, were flying the short-nosed fighter variant of the Blenheim, the Mark 1F. I knew, of course, that in 1935 the prototype Blenheim had proved faster than any of the current RAF fighters, but that by the time it saw service, with so many weighty modifications incorporated, it was outclassed by all the German fighters. But while discounting so daunting a fact I still resented being separated from the other – shorter – chaps I had joined up with. True enough, as the losses on the Defiant squadrons soared I had to accept that the posting had, in fact, been something of a gift of life.

My airborne station on the Blenheim was the mid-upper turret which, on our machines, had a single 0.303 inch (7.7 mm) calibre Vickers machine gun. Additionally the pilot had a forward-firing capability (unlike on the Defiant) using four 0.303 Brownings augmented by another single wing-mounted Browning. The turret was cold and windy and was held to be statistically unhealthy, despite which – the proof being in the pudding – at least six of our gunners not only survived the war but lived on past the millennium. Doughty old Howard Duart reached a hale ninety-nine!

As aircraftman air gunners we wore the AG brevet, although I had managed to obtain one of the coveted, but even then superseded, brass flying-bullet arm badges. Then, in May 1940, it was ruled that all non-commissioned aircrew should be sergeants, a development which, understandably, was poorly received by non-aircrew personnel.

The 'Flying Bullet' arm badge.

Although our home station was Catterick we operated from forward bases at Leeming and West Hartlepool, as the Battle of Britain developed.

The Battle is now reckoned to have lasted from 10 July to 31 October 1940, and certainly, I was operational on the Greatest Day – 15 August, when the most ever Luftwaffe sorties were launched – except that, owing to an oxygen fault, we landed after fifteen minutes. My own busiest period, however, came towards the end of the month when I flew on fifteen sorties in three days. Looking back I remember becoming aware that while I had the mental capacity to treat the pressure of what we were doing as routine I still grew extremely tired.

Ironically, my most hazardous moment during the Battle was on 11 October 1940, during a night-flying test over London. It was a moonlit night when we saw these three fighters, only to relax as we identified them as Spitfires. But then, as they approached, the two wing men peeled off to the right and left respectively, leaving the leader to bore straight in at us. We saw the flashes then, and suddenly bullets were pattering like hail on our metal roof.

Fortunately, although all three in turn ran in, none of the attacks was pressed too closely and we did not have to open fire. It transpired that the Spitfires were manned by Polish pilots. Certainly, at the time, the questions went all the way up the chain of command and then down again, but I see that my logbook records the encounter, politically, undoubtedly, as a 'mock attack' by Spitfires.

This after-dark encounter notwithstanding, as daytime Blenheim losses increased, so night operations became the norm. Our war job during this period, required us to engage enemy bombers – or to obstruct them, at least – while avoiding confrontations with their fighter escorts. I maintain, therefore, that by simply being a damn nuisance to German aircraft on their way to bomb Britain – indeed by our very presence showing that we were not simply lying down and taking it – we shouldered our load alongside all the high-scoring Hurricane and Spitfire aces during that so-decisive battle.

After a while the squadron – No. 219 Squadron still – moved to RAF Redhill in Surrey, where I continued to operate the Blenheim but also the AI-equipped Beaufighter (AI being airborne-interception radar). The radar gave us a double boost, for not only did it enable us to track down enemy bombers at night but the darkness made it unlikely that they would have a fighter escort. Again, my station was a dorsal turret with either a single Vickers K machine gun (gas operated and very rapid firing, at 1,200 rounds a minute) or a single Browning. Additionally, however, the aircraft had four nose-mounted 20 mm cannon and six wing-mounted 0.303 inch (7.7 mm) calibre machine guns.

Regarding the AI radar, in those early days it was pretty much left to us to learn to use it, only later would it become the subject of a dedicated operational training unit course. The technique employed was that ground-controlled radar would direct us into an area where German aircraft were seen to be operating. We would then be instructed to switch on our equipment – 'Flash your weapon' – after which I would take over.

Any aircraft would display on each of my twin, three-inch screens as a blip, but a friendly machine would be expected to show an Identification-Friend-or-Foe signal (IFF) beside its blip. If no IFF signal was seen then I would direct the pilot as the occasion

A Bristol Beaufighter, with the early Air Interception, pre-scanner, aerials at the nose.

demanded, 'Climb, and turn right', for example, until the target was held in the centre crosses on my scopes. I would then tell him to look ahead. As we caught up he would make visual contact, positively identify the quarry as an enemy and commence an attack.

The job could be very frustrating, the early AI being so temperamental that only too often it would break down, forcing us to abort the sortie. 'Returning to base,' I would call disgustedly, explaining – employing the prescribed procedural phrase – 'my weapon is bent.' A format which delighted the WAAF operators who would sympathise, 'Poor Gregory, his weapon is bent again.'

Of course, as time went on so we became more experienced and the AI itself increased in both sophistication and effectiveness – not least in employing a single scope. After I left the squadron two colleagues, Terry Clarke and his pilot, grew very adept, downing six enemy aircraft and being decorated for their prowess.

As I have indicated, the deterrent role we had undertaken to date had been gratifying enough but with AI we truly took our place among the warriors, as is shown by a section of the Combat-in-the-Air report my pilot, Flt Lt Dottridge, and I submitted on 12 March 1941:

> (The crew were) first controlled by Beetle, then Flintlock. Ordered to 10,000 feet on 190° until 6 miles SSE of Selsey Bill. The AI got a blip but the hostile outstripped them at mid-Channel, and they were ordered back. A second contact was made, but this hostile escaped at low altitude. A series of vectors then gave a third contact.

The aircraft was descended through 6,000 feet, the pilot making visual contact just south of Brighton. The hostile took evasive action but an attack was pressed home – despite fire from the enemy's rear gunner – resulting in a flash, and then smoke from its right engine, together with some debris. The hostile – a Ju88, the pilot thought – descended steeply towards the sea and was claimed as destroyed. The official Fighter Command verdict, however, was "One EA [enemy aircraft], unidentified, Probable".

In fact, my logbook entry for that night reads 'One enemy aircraft engaged, Heinkel One-Eleven, believed destroyed'. And when the wreckage of a Heinkel 111 was subsequently found I was able to add a note, 'Confirmed'. The encounter alone had been a great boost to our morale so we were ecstatic to have the kill confirmed.

In March 1941 I was posted to Blackpool to complete the wireless operating element of my dual role, the ensuing six weeks being largely spent in brushing up on my morse. I was then posted to Yatesbury, in Wiltshire, for a final polish in airborne operating of both wireless and AI, after which I was able to add a radio flash to my sleeve, showing that I was now fully trained both as an air gunner and a wireless operator. I then returned to the squadron in the capacity of Radio Observer, a security title designed to cover up the radar element of my function.

A Douglas Boston Light Bomber.

I found the squadron at Tangmere, near Chichester, on the South Coast, only to be told that I was now overqualified for my previous role, so that in November 1941 I was posted again, this time to No. 23 Squadron, at nearby Ford.

My new squadron, I discovered, were flying Bostons on night-intruder operations, the sorties being carried out for the most part over Northern France. During such sorties, however, most of my new operating skills went to waste, for to obviate interception by German direction-finding stations we were forbidden to transmit. As for receiving information – weather deterioration warnings, in the main – although in training we had achieved a morse-reading speed of twenty-four words a minute, messages were now sent at just eight words a minute. This was to ensure that the aircraft wireless operator, often bouncing about the sky at low level, received the strictly one-off transmission correctly and had no need to even think of asking for a repetition.

Night-intruder ops had already proved full of interest, when, in December 1941, we received an extended brief authorising us to disrupt German operations whenever and wherever possible. At times this saw us directed to attack specific targets. For the most part, though, it gave us a roving commission to attack whatever took our fancy: in essence, doing anything to make life difficult for the German occupying forces. In accomplishing this we would gaily range over Northern France, Belgium and Holland strafing and bombing trains, vehicles, marshalling yards, factories; indeed anything that offered.

A quirk of the job was that as we set out from our south coast bases, wave-hopping to carry out a sweep in France, we would often cross with our opposite numbers, similarly holding low to engage in a sweep over Britain. Indeed, not a few times we would return to find that our base had been bombed, necessitating a diversion to an undamaged airfield.

My regular pilot on Bostons was my squadron commander, Squadron Leader Bertie Rex O'Bryen Hoare. Earlier in his flying career an engine panel had blown back in flight and damaged his right eye, an injury which, strangely enough, had vastly improved its night vision. In all, we were to carry out thirty-two operational sweeps as a crew.

Rear-facing view of a strafed convoy as two soldiers (just above the tail) seek cover.

Squadron Leader Bertie Rex O'Bryen Hoare, DSO and Bar, DFC and Bar.

The general pattern of our ops was that we'd hold low over the Channel to avoid radars, then pull up to tree-top level as we crossed the coast. Later, once our stint was done, the return to base was invariably made by letting down to wave-hop once again. During such sweeps searchlights and anti-aircraft installations were often bothersome but we rarely saw enemy fighters. As for the work itself, although, as I have said, we had free licence to attack whatever we liked, Bertie normally kept our bombs for aircraft surprised at their dispersals.

On occasion, Bertie, with his damaged eye and superb handlebar moustache, would display a truly Nelsonic brand of leadership. This characteristic came to the fore when I received a bad-weather recall message – our decoding instructions for such communications, issued for each sortie, were printed on edible rice paper! Having been passed the recall order, however, Bertie made a tactical decision and decided to carry on with the sortie. Naturally, the recall having been in the form of an order, I demurred. At which he demanded, 'You haven't acknowledged receiving it, have you?' With radio silence being the rule, of course, he knew fine well I hadn't. 'Well then,' he said. And at debriefing, had it been queried, he would undoubtedly have protested, with blandly angelic regret, 'We saw no signal'.

My logbook entry for 3 April 1942, therefore, is not typical of the press-on spirit that then existed, reading, 'Boston Mk.3, Night Intruder, Dinard, weather NBG [no bloody good] returned and diverted West Malling, two hours ten minutes.'

In July 1942 I was detached to RAF Sutton Bridge, Lincolnshire, for a six-week gunnery leaders' course. And on 28 August 1942 my fiancée Edith and I were married at Boulton St Mary, Derby, honeymooning for the rest of my snatched leave in Castleton.

Edith and I had known each other since 1938, having met at a dance in Alvaston, near Derby, where we both lived. Although she had a civilian job she would travel to visit me as often as she could, always pestering me to get married. Being on ops I did not think that would be a good thing, and so I tried to put her off. But it was not to be, and once I had given up the fight in 1942 we were to be together for another 57 years. She really was that persistent!

At the time I was an acting warrant officer, but a month or two after my return Bertie summoned me to his office and asked if I had thought of taking a commission. He spent some time pointing out the disadvantages of relinquishing my lofty warrant officer rank to become a lowly pilot officer. But having pointed out the pitfalls – the loss of status and the drop in pay – he recommended me. After which, without any further interviews, my commission was approved, being promulgated on 11 November 1942.

The supporting papers, I see, unearthing them for the purpose, record, 'Recommended by the commander of No. 605 Squadron, Wing Commander G.H. Dunholm, and by station commander F. Maxwell MC DFC AFC: "Gregory is an excellent type...".' The final approving signature was that of the Air Marshal Commanding No. 11 Group, the celebrated R. Leigh-Mallory, who wrote, '[Gregory is] An intelligent type of airman who has proved himself to be a competent and reliable wireless operator/air gunner. He has done good work on operations'. And that was it. There was no 'knife-fork-and-spoon' course [Officer Cadet Training Unit course], merely a money grant to cover a tailored uniform and kit.

A short while later, however, Bertie was posted from No. 23 Squadron onto Mosquitos, and as these did not require a dedicated gunner we had to part company. Just the same, having assumed command of RAF Little Snoring, in Norfolk, Bertie seems to have missed me – or at least, my name – for he promptly found himself a second A. E. Gregory! Another officer, but a navigator this time, my namesake's prowess being recorded alongside Bertie's on a plaque in Little Snoring's village church.

In fact, Bertie went on to survive the war but was killed on 26 March 1947 when his Mosquito crashed in the course of a delivery flight to New Zealand. When he died he was a thirty-five year old wing commander on No. 84 Squadron, with a DSO and bar and a DFC and bar.

As for me, my DFC appeared in the *London Gazette* on 13 July 1943, the award being conferred, according to the citation, for 'Long and meritorious service as an air gunner, having been engaged in night flying for nearly three years'. I blush to see that it also commended what it called my 'great courage, skill, and devotion to duty'. In truth, looking back over my own wartime operational flying and thinking about such concepts as courage, I suppose I was always pragmatic. Certainly, I never felt fear, never found myself engaged at a personal level and was, therefore, always able to surmount any downturns.

By that time, after all, I'd done thirty-two ops with Bertie, hadn't got hurt, and hadn't had to bale out. It was self-evident, then, that I was getting away with it. Of course, we were losing people, many of them, but I didn't want to come off ops. Not least because I noticed that those who came off only rarely got back on again.

In September 1942, therefore, when No. 23 Squadron itself converted to Mosquitos, I organised myself a transfer to No. 605 Squadron, back along the coast to Tangmere, and did ten more Boston night-intruder ops with them. But when No. 605 too went onto Mosquitos there were mutterings about my coming off ops. In fact, I was told outright, 'You've done far too much. It's an operational training unit for you.'

Still feeling invincible, and even more determined not to be grounded, I got myself onto No. 275 Squadron at RAF Valley, Anglesey, and flew on, carrying out air/sea rescue work on Ansons and Lysanders, also on Walrus amphibians. Here, the primary task was to patrol the Welsh coast and Irish Sea, to locate ditched crews with the Anson or Lysander, then to summon a Walrus amphibian to effect the rescue.

The air/sea rescue work continued when I was posted to RAF Woolsington, Northumberland, but now with patrols covering the North Sea and South Coast. Then, in May 1944, I transferred to the newly formed No. 278 Squadron at RAF Martlesham Heath, re-locating with it in February 1945 to RAF Thorney Island near Portsmouth. During my stay on this squadron we relinquished some of our aircraft types, finally settling with the Walrus and Sea Otter.

When the war ended I applied to remain in the RAF but the vast overmanning precluded this and on 31 December 1945 I returned to the Co-op's transport division, to find it little enough changed, if now motorised.

Only too soon, however, civilian life palled, and I set about returning to the RAF. Air gunners were no longer needed but I succeeding in obtaining an Extended Service Commission as a flight lieutenant air signaller-cum-loadmaster, re-entering the Service in May 1947.

After some refresher training in the wireless operating role, and having undergone an air loadmaster's course, I was posted to the Far East Air Force to join No. 52 Squadron, then located at RAF Changi, Singapore. The squadron was equipped with Dakotas to fulfil the twofold task of flying the area's routes and carrying out jungle supply-dropping operations in support of the ongoing Malayan Emergency.

The route flying took us all around the Far Eastern theatre, but lack of local servicing facilities alone meant periodically flying the aircraft to Australia for scheduled checks: necessary but wasteful jaunts entailing three weeks away from base and some sixty

The Douglas DC-3, the Dakota, to the RAF.

hours squandered off the aircraft's availability (thirty out and thirty back)! These aside, among my 'specials' I logged a ferry flight to New Zealand, carrying a replacement engine for an unserviceable VIP aircraft.

Among our bread and butter schedules, during which my function was to maintain communications, were flights to Hong Kong, which involved a refuelling stop in Saigon, in what was then French Indo-China. As this was an active war zone we weren't allowed to leave the vicinity of the aircraft and were obliged to carry revolvers. As indeed we were when engaged in our other role, that of dropping supplies to patrols operating in the Malayan jungle.

For this task, one of the three transport squadrons in the theatre would move to a grass strip near Kuala Lumpur, each squadron covering the duty for three months and sending up at least one of its flights depending upon the requirement at the time. When carrying out these operations, roller tracks would be fitted to the floor and the cargo door detached and left on the ground. The pilot and navigator would map-read to the dropping zone and at the sound of our engines the expectant troops would send up a smoke signal.

On such operational drops the signaller not only did the communications but doubled as the loadmaster-cum-air-despatcher (despatch, with an e, being the approved spelling in this context at that time!). This meant that he was responsible for loading the supply-packs – the rollers made it easier to hump the packs while airborne – then, once over the dropping zone, for throwing them and their parachutes out through the open cargo door. I say parachutes, although many packs at that time were free dropped. The packs having gone, the signaller, now secured by a webbing safety strap, would lean out, craning back into the airflow in order to report to the pilot how close to the marker panel they had fallen. 'Right, Greg,' mine would respond succinctly. And if they were not that accurate he would scrape the treetops even closer on the next circuit.

Although the signaller nearly always handled the despatching himself, there were occasions on which we would take an airman aboard to help. In fact, in later days, four-man Air Despatcher (the 'e' again!) crews from the Royal Army Service Corps would take over the rear-fuselage role for both supply and leaflet dropping. In my day, though, we air signaller-cum-loadmasters were it.

Jungle supply dropping in such hilly terrain was demanding work with many potential dangers. Indeed, in the course of the Emergency it was to cost several aircraft and crews. Certainly, it kept us busy so that in July and August 1950, when I carried out thirteen and fifteen operational supply drops respectively, it was my busiest time since the Battle of Britain.

During my tour a family emergency necessitated my making the hastiest possible return to the UK. Gaining the necessary compassionate leave presented no problem,

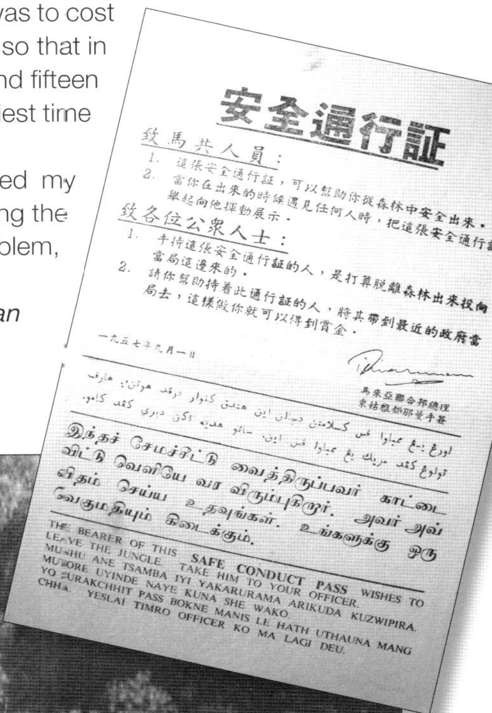

安全通行証

致馬共人員：

1. 這張安全通行証，可以幫助你從森林中安全出來。
2. 當你在出來的時候遇見任何人時，把這張安全通行証舉起向他揮動展示。

致各位公衆人士：

1. 手持這張安全通行証的人，是打算脫離森林出來投向當局這邊來的。
2. 請你幫助持着此通行証的人，將其帶到最近的政府當局去，這樣做你就可以得到賞金。

一九五七年九月一日

馬來亞聯合邦總理
東姑鴨都拉曼手簽

இந்தச் செமத்சிட்டு வைத்திருப்பவர் காட்டை விட்டு வெளியே வர விரும்புகிறார். அவர் அவ் விதம் செய்ய உதவுங்கள். உங்களுக்கு ஒரு வெகுமதியும் கிடைக்கும்.

THE BEARER OF THIS SAFE CONDUCT PASS WISHES TO LEAVE THE JUNGLE. TAKE HIM TO YOUR OFFICER.
MUSHU ANE TSAMBA IYI YAKARURAMA ARIKUDA KUZWIPIRA.
MUTORE UYINDE NAYE KUNA SHE WAKO.
YO SURAKCHHIT PASS BOKNE MANIS LE HATH UTHAUNA MANG CHHA. YESLAI TIMRO OFFICER KO MA LAGI DEU.

A safe-conduct leaflet, dropped during the Malayan Emergency.

'Pack away!' jungle supply dropping.

for while the ailing relative was alive the return home rated top priority. The flight, though, costed at £525, represented the price of a small house! Fortunately, the British Legion stepped in to stand the expense. Of course, in coming back to the Far East after that leave I had to endure the troopship's 28-day passage, a journey which Edith also suffered when coming out to join me a little later on.

It really was a most enjoyable tour, but eventually it came to an end and in October 1950 the troopship *Orduna* took us back to the UK.

My next posting was to No. 6 Flying Training School at RAF Ternhill, Shropshire, as both chief signals instructor and assistant chief ground instructor. That appointment was followed by one to No. 1 Air Signallers' School at RAF Swanton Morley, Norfolk, again as chief signals instructor. After that my final posting was to the School of Recruit Training at RAF Hednesford, near Lichfield, where, as assistant adjutant and flight commander, I was responsible for drill and general service training.

Three ground postings on the trot! But during them I had maintained my flying status – and my flying pay! – by getting airborne once a month in such types as Tiger Moths and Chipmunks. However, having logged my last flight at the end of December 1954, I duly left the RAF in May 1955.

By the end of my service my logbook recorded that I had flown 2,165 hours; 1,900 by day, and 296 by night. Of this total 587 hours had been operational, comprising 317 wartime hours (sixty-two operational sweeps) and 270 hours during the Malayan Emergency (ninety-one operational supply dropping sorties).

Additionally, during the Malayan tour, and having completed the specified, 'Ten years exemplary service in the auxiliary and volunteer air forces of the United Kingdom and Commonwealth', I had been honoured with the Air Efficiency Award.

But awards, with me, were never to be a straightforward issue. The Defence Medal, for example, was not ticked off on my initial issue of campaign medals, but mulling over the conditions for its award in 2003 (some 57 years on!) I wrote to the RAF Records Office to claim it. The Personnel Management Agency at RAF Innsworth wrote back to confirm that I did indeed qualify for this essentially non-combatant award, but – rather mystifyingly – 'by virtue of having won the DFC'!

On a sort of similar head, although I actually took part in the 1953 Coronation Parade – not only commanding a street-lining detachment but even saluting with my shiny sword! – my name failed to come up in the draw for Coronation Medals.

What was truly chagrining, however, was a 2005 initiative by the Malaysian government when they decided to issue an especially struck medal for those who, sixty years earlier, had paved the way for their independence. For the Malaysian powers-that-be set qualifying dates that actually excluded me and all those others who were involved in the rough, tough, early days of the Emergency!

Medals awarded to Flight Lieutenant Albert Gregory: (left to right) - Distinguished Flying Cross; 1939-45 Star, with Battle of Britain Clasp; Air Crew Europe Star, with Atlantic Clasp; Defence Medal;War Medal 1939-45; General Service Medal, with Clasp Malaya;Air Efficiency Award.

But for many years all such Service-related matters went into abeyance as Edith and I busied ourselves running a grocer's shop in Alvaston, Derby. Only having retired, and more especially after 1999, when I found myself widowed, did I have space to turn my mind back to my RAF days. Once I had done so, however, I found myself increasingly involved.

From 1980 to 2003, for example, I was among the veterans of the Battle of Britain who were annually honoured by the United States Air Force at the American-garrisoned RAF stations of Alconbury and Lakenheath. Then there were the annual Battle of Britain reunions centred upon Bentley Priory with an associated service at Westminster Abbey. In more recent years I attended the dedication ceremonies for the memorials at Folkestone's Capel Le Ferne and London's Victoria Embankment. There have also been group and squadron functions when my attendance has been graciously eased by the provision of transport. Then again, there are the venues – sometimes at airshows – where a group of us are brought together and the public come to have us sign items for them. And they come in their droves!

One associated singularity: many years back I donated my senior NCO's tunic as a fund raiser for the RAF Benevolent Fund. In 2007, long after I had forgotten having done so, I was contacted by a would-be eBay purchaser who wanted to establish the tunic's authenticity: almost full circle for my antediluvian AG brevet and wireless flash, from trailing aerials and morse code to an offshoot of the world-wide web!

All that aside, the years, of course, continue to take their inexorable toll of The Few, but I like to feel that in some measure I represent the spirit of those 3,000 or so pilots and aircrew who, during those desperate days, refused to be beaten by the odds. Certainly the most prized of my wartime awards is the Battle of Britain clasp.

Former Flight Lieutenant Gregory at the September 2005 inauguration of the Battle of Britain Memorial on Victoria Embankment.

7

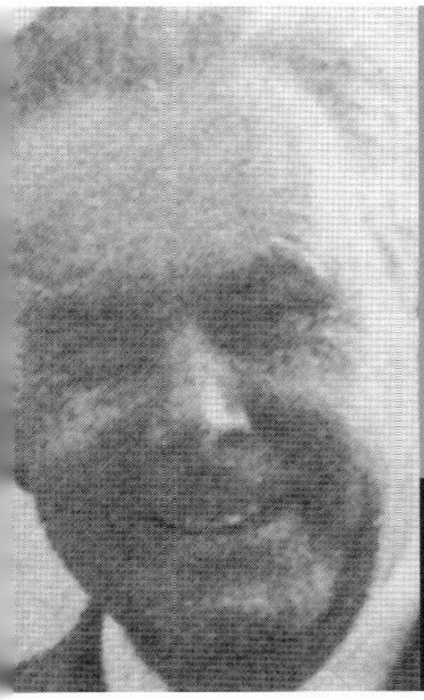

A Truly Gallant Airman

Wing Commander Donald George Southwell, DFM
wireless operator/air gunner

In 1940 Mr Donald Southwell, an office manager with a facility for statistics, was twenty-eight, married, had two children, and was living in Gravesend. In 1981 he committed his early wartime experiences to paper, entitling the manuscript, self-deprecatingly, *The Ungallant Airman*, from which, with unbounded respect, this account is adapted. Mr Southwell died in January 1989.

As a boy I had spent a lot of time at Gravesend Airport, often imagining a catastrophe from which I would emerge as a hero to the applause of adulating bystanders. Little wonder then, that six months into the war, I volunteered to fly as a pilot in the RAF, though with limited expectation of heroics. For hadn't Miss Phillips, years back in Infants, told our class, 'Always remember that one Briton is worth ten of any other race'. And as she also taught us that two and two is four, and as – being adept at figures – I had found her to be right in that case, I had no reason to doubt her in regarding the Germans as less than worthy opponents.

My medical caused me some problems. Indeed, in separating colours and lights – the red light did not register – I actually cheated, besides being frugal with the truth regarding migraines and other areas of my history. But finally, by arguing my corner, I was accepted, albeit grudgingly – 'you've just scraped through' – not for pilot, but for wireless operator/air gunner.

Four weeks later I began my radio-qualifying training at Blackpool. The greatest hurdle of the six-month course was reaching the required facility – 18 to 20 words a minute – with the dits and dohs of the morse code. Here, in a strange reversal of what I came to realise was the norm, I found it easy enough to receive messages but laboured to reach the demanded sending speed!

Next came a gunnery course at Jurby, on the Isle of Man, during which I achieved a rare distinction by shooting a hole in the tail of my own aircraft instead of in the target drogue. However, everyone who was anyone was adamant that restrictive stops made it impossible for even the most inept trainee gunner to hit his own tail, arguing that the shot must, therefore, have come from another aircraft. As I was only too ready to go along with this majority view, that particular distinction never did get aired for adulation.

Having left Jurby as a sergeant entitled to wear both an AG (air gunners) brevet and a wireless flash, there was a period of home leave before a further course at No. 10 Operational Training Unit at Abingdon, near Oxford, where I honed my wireless-operating and air-gunnery skills on Ansons. Finally, now deemed fully trained, I was posted to Dishforth, in Yorkshire, to No. 10 Squadron, at that time operating war-battered and by then obsolescent Whitleys.

As it happened, I found myself effectively 'surplus to requirements' at Dishforth, but the time I spent awaiting re-posting gave me the opportunity to take stock. In particular, I found myself dwelling upon the number of beds left vacant after any operation. Left vacant, moreover, by young chaps I had been talking to and drinking with only hours before. With my facility for statistics I applied myself to working out the odds on my surviving the required thirty operations, coming to the inescapable conclusion that I could not last longer than four, and possibly even three, trips.

But before I could reach any real conclusion, and certainly before I could decide upon a course of action, I was sent to Linton-on-Ouse, Yorkshire, to join No. 35 Squadron, presently engaged in bringing the Halifax four-engined bomber into service. And just days later my name appeared on the battle order.

My first operational flight was to Essen, taking the mid-upper gunner's position. Until then I had never known what fear was. On the outbound leg I tried to detach myself by contemplating the stars, taking comfort from their remoteness, and from a belief that there was little likelihood of fighters or searchlights finding our aircraft in that immensity. This complacent reflection was shattered, however, by a burst of anti-aircraft fire.

A Handley Page Halifax Mk.2.

Startled, I inadvertently triggered my turret's four Browning machine guns, bringing an instant 'Fighter-attack!' alarm from our rear gunner. 'They were close, Skipper,' he amplified, 'the tracers went just above my turret.' I realised that he was merely misinterpreting my finger-twitch but I didn't dare admit to what I'd done. I just shut my eyes and waited, and when all was quiet again, gasped a sigh of relief.

In the ensuing period of calm I tried to persuade myself that the stories I had heard from other aircrew were exaggerated. After all, this encounter with flak hadn't been that bad. But the respite was short lived, for just minutes later we were engulfed by what seemed to me like a sheet of fire and flames. At which I tried to get out of the turret. Only to have my parachute harness snag on a projection and prevent me from leaving. As it was, by the time I had freed myself we had flown out of that hazard too.

Then came the approach to the target with the pilot having to jink about to avoid searchlights. Eventually, though, we dropped our bombs and turned for home. And aeons later, as it seemed to me, landed safely. Once back in the billet, however, I got into bed and pulled the covers over my head, desperate to try and blot out the night's events.

I awoke early. To find nine empty beds among the thirty the billet contained. So much for head burying! For having registered the significance of such a toll, and then by daily refinements of my calculations – the operations programme being relentless – I was left with a current casualty rate of from twenty to twenty-five per cent.

With this very much on my mind I became acquainted with another aircrew sergeant who, over drinks at the bar, confessed to having similar misgivings about his chances of survival. Of course, as all aircrew are volunteers, getting ourselves removed from flying was merely a matter of reporting to the squadron office. But this had ramifications. The immediate loss of one's stripes, for a start, which meant a serious loss of pay. Additionally it meant the ignominy of being charged with cowardice, with 'lack of moral fibre' (LMF). The only way out was to be honourably stood down.

It had come to me, days since, that my best line of action was to confess to the station medical officer that my lifelong bane, ophthalmic migraine, deliberately concealed at my medical board, had returned to make my life hell. That would do the trick. For an air gunner suddenly overcome by a migraine aura would be a serious liability to the rest of his crew. As would a wireless operator whose thudding head could well blot out what might be a lifesaving signal.

I trotted all this out over a beer or two, but my confidant seemed unimpressed, remaining sceptical, even though I described to him in great detail just how debilitating my migraine attacks could be.

But he was not a true sceptic, for just days later he was stood down from flying duties, having described to the medical officer exactly how those untraceable effects I

A partly camouflage-netted Tirpitz *sheltering near Trondheirm in February 1942.*

had described were affecting his duty! Not only that, he had pleaded for treatment that would enable him to carry on flying until he had completed his tour! His subtlety paid off, for him, but his treacherous purloining of my own, genuine case, I felt, had disbarred me from using it.

In the interim I had flown several more ops, including a petrifying, flak-filled trip to Cologne where I had shivered and cowered at the wireless set for most of the way there and a good proportion of the way back. At that, though, sitting hunched at the wireless, blind to the outside world, was marginally better than seeing it all from the turret.

Then, on 27 April 1942, we were sent to carry out a low-level attack on the *Tirpitz*, at that time sheltering under the cliffs in Norway's Foetten Fiord. We duly completed the sortie, and suffered accordingly.

Even then, although we inflicted damage, it was only slight and the vessel was moved, leaving the job to be done all over again. Nor was it any comfort to me when our commanding officer, Wing Commander Bennett, later of Pathfinder and civil-airline fame, who had been shot down on the raid, evaded via Sweden and returned to his command after an absence of just five weeks.

In the aftermath of all this we were visited by Winston Churchill! But although his buoyancy renewed a little of my pre-ops zeal, it swiftly evaporated a few night's later when sixteen of our billet's thirty beds were emptied. Even for a non-statistician that would have taken some living with.

By 19 May 1942 I had logged forty hours flying and eight ops. For my ninth, our seven-man crew was dispatched to raid Mannheim with a mixed load of incendiaries and high explosives.

The crew comprised: Flying Officer Ronald Walter Valters, pilot; Sergeant Sidney Richard Stickney, second pilot; Pilot Officer R.G. Baker, navigator; Sergeant William Richard Hunt, flight engineer; Sergeant George Daft, mid-upper gunner; me, as wireless operator/air gunner; and Flight Sergeant Gordon Kennedy, Royal Canadian Air Force, rear gunner.

Flak caught us as we crossed the French coast, but after checking around the captain carried on for the target. A little later, taking shelter, as it were, he slotted in behind a Lancaster which was taking the attention of both flak and a cone of searchlights. I was horrified, therefore, to see the other aircraft suddenly dissolve in a great, rapidly-fading orange glow. It was a sight that so unnerved me that all I could do was reflect upon the souls of the chaps who had just been blown to perdition and wonder, in a case like that, how the Almighty would ever put the pieces together again.

Shocked beyond measure, I swept the frequency dial seeking anything to distract me. Then I heard Vera Lynn. And that helped, for her calm, sweet tones transported me to a world far removed from the one in which aircraft just like ours could instantly metamorphose into balls of flame.

We droned steadily onwards. Until the calm was shattered by an engine-drowning burst of noise, our aircraft shuddering to multiple impacts as a night-fighter pressed home its attack.

'Jesus, that was close!' It was Gordon, from the rear turret.

Both close and gut-wrenching as we began to corkscrew. But moments later our attacker let fly at us again, a flash from the port wing lighting up my compartment as the fuselage flooded with smoke.

'Feather the port inner,' I heard the skipper call to the second pilot, followed instantly by, 'Christ, man, you've feathered the port outer!' At which, with two engines dead, the aircraft heeled over on one wing, then stalled and began to spiral earthwards, the skipper ordering, just moments later, 'Bale out, chaps, I can't hold her.'

Grabbing my parachute and snapping it to my chest, I managed to get to an escape hatch and not without difficulty evacuated the aircraft. My parachute deployed successfully but the descent was swift, and when the canopy snagged upon a tree I was spilled headfirst onto a metalled road.

After laying immobile for a while I struggled from my harness, only then becoming aware that my head was streaming blood and that much of the skin had gone from my left hand. Investigating further I saw that my left trouser leg was split and the knee bone itself exposed. The initial feeling of relief at having survived gave way to one of black despair. There was no sound, and no sign of anyone else. Where our Halifax had landed, and whether anyone else had got out, who could say!

And at that moment, when I was at my lowest ebb, and only just beginning to collect myself, it came to me that the first signs of the dawn now showing, grey and spiritless as it was, heralded my tenth wedding anniversary!

Some guide to my state of mind can be gathered from the fact that, having secreted my parachute in a ditch, I negotiated a pole-barrier across the road and saw a sign declaiming 'Pratt's Ethyl Petrol'; from which I concluded that I must be in England. Another notice, just yards further on, this one in German, soon put me right. I was to find, in fact, that I had come down at Nouzonville, in Champagne-Ardenne, and that the barrier marked the Franco-Belgian frontier.

I continued to stagger on. I had heard stories of escape lines, and formed a vague purpose of trying to find one.

My first attempt was far from auspicious. A man in a beret came in sight. Collapsing onto the grass I waited until he neared me then, in what French I had, I explained that I was a British airman who, as an ally, claimed the right to his assistance. At which he gave a shocked jump – conceivably at my accent – and made off.

Then a woman approached. Sinking onto the grass again, I repeated my spiel.

'I don't believe you are British,' she told me. 'I believe you are German, and trying to trap me.' Then, suddenly unbending, 'You poor boy!' she cried.

For a moment I felt that my cares were over. But it was not to be.

'I'm afraid I can't help you,' she said. 'However,' she pointed ahead, 'that is Nouzonville. There will be no Germans in it until later. But there is a café on the main street where you might get assistance.'

No Germans, but before reaching the café I had grown a tail of thirty or forty sympathetic-looking, if largely silent, people! The patron and his wife ushered me into a waiting chair.

Coffee was proffered, and how welcome it was! And then came a whole succession of people out to view, mostly women, many tearful, some of whom set about tending my cuts and bruises.

After a while, the first lady came in, her face sober. 'I have heard about your aeroplane,' she told me. 'I am afraid there are at least four or five bodies in the wreckage. It came down near Aiglemont, about five kilometres north-east of Charleville-Mèziéres. Fortunately it is deep in the forest and unlikely to be found by the Germans for some time yet.'

However, as off-duty Germans were expected to arrive from their camp at nearby

Mèziéres, I was escorted from the town and set down on a wooded hillside. I felt rather aggrieved at being kicked out, but to stay in town, I was assured, was impossible. And there, with a bottle of wine and a sandwich or two, I was left to my own devices.

The next three or four days as I made my way through the woods have never been anything but hazy. On one occasion I awoke from a fitful sleep to find four German soldiers, their rifles set aside, lolling on a nearby bank, smoking and showing each other photographs. Hurriedly collecting my wits, I kept low and very quiet indeed, and after a while they shambled off.

My limbs had long stiffened up and progress was daily becoming steadily more laborious when I heard French voices calling repeatedly, 'Comrade? Comrade?'

Having revealed myself I was told to make my way to a nearby house. It was where I was to be hidden, I learnt, but I was directed to wait thirty minutes before making my way there. In truth, I felt too weak to walk another step but they had plied me with a liquor so fiery that it set me going once again.

Having arrived, my first knock brought no answer, but then the door swung back and I was ushered into a room full of expectant faces. At a loss, I gazed around, announced, 'Winston Churchill will be told of this' and gave the V-for-Victory salute. At this everyone smiled. And it was V-signs all around. After a while a hot bath was prepared for me, but the moment I was shown a bed, I fell asleep.

It was a week before a doctor could be fetched from Mèziéres to examine my knee. Surgery, he decided, was unnecessary, but he advocated much more rest. Ten days later, however, I persuaded my hosts to allow me to hobble downstairs so that I could begin getting mobile once again.

By then I had learnt that the four of my crew so far accounted for had been buried with full military honours near Nouzonville; that there was still no news of Pilot Officer Baker, the navigator, or of Sergeant George Daft, the mid-upper gunner.

Then, just after I was able to get about, and when my host and his family were in the fields, a truck carrying two Germans pulled up outside the house. I ran upstairs and hid under a bed. After which I spent the most uncomfortable twenty minutes ever. Getting no answer to their knocks, the soldiers entered, then 'halloing' their way from room to room, carried out a search, even – by the sound of the hatch cover falling back – peering up into the loft.

They departed shortly afterwards, but I was left very shaken, and when my hosts returned with the news that house-to-house searches were being carried out throughout the area I could not bring myself to tell them that their house too, remote as it was, had been searched. Silly, I know, but I thought it might worry them more to know of my – of *their* – lucky escape. For, to be found harbouring me meant the death penalty for my hosts. Clearly it was time I moved on.

If any Germans stop us … What our passeurs *– our escorting patriots – braved daily.*

Co-incidentally, the very next day I was photographed wearing a beret, and just hours later, handed an identity card which showed that I was Pierre Jean Mercier, of No.10 Place du Capitol, Toulouse.

Three weeks after they had taken me in, my hosts held a party for me. And early next morning a van arrived. 'We go to Mèziéres,' the driver briefed. 'It is a garrison town, so if any Germans stop us, you must say that you begged a lift. That I don't know you otherwise.' Which, I suppose, was fair enough, if unsettling.

In fact, we reached Mèziéres without incident. Having parked, the driver then led me through the streets, instructing me: 'Keep twenty metres behind…' and having delivered me to an imposing looking house, vanished.

I spent just one night here. The plan, I was told, was to move me further from the crash. Accordingly, next morning the lady of the house took me to the railway station

Throughout Occupied Europe, the civil population is warned against giving aid to evaders and escaping POWs.

where she purchased two tickets for Amagne, some thirty kilometres off. Slipping me one of them, she then walked ahead of me and entered a carriage. German soldiers were checking tickets but only stopping every few passengers. I had a horrible moment when they stopped the woman ahead of me but they took no notice of me as I sidled past, selected the carriage behind my guide's, and tried to quell my heartbeats.

There was more trauma at Amagne, where soldiers were eyeing every passenger, but steeling myself I brazened it out and walked on unchallenged. Once outside the station, and following instructions again, I trailed my guide until she stopped at a second-hand book shop and briefly engaged a man in conversation. She then turned back for the station, pointedly ignoring me as she passed.

The man proved to be her husband's brother who, having bussed both my cheeks enthusiastically, told me that my next stop was to be a café at Aussonce. The only snag was that it would mean a twenty kilometre bike ride: and a fixed-wheel bike, at that! Suffice to say that my knee gave me gyp from the start.

As before, I was to follow, not closing with my guide. But after a while, he let me catch up with him.

'When will the Second Front come?' he demanded.

'Er,' I gasped, 'I don't know.' But having learnt how much store was put upon this eventuality, I suggested, 'Perhaps two years or so?'

He grunted, turned about again, then pedalled furiously away, leaving me to catch up as best I could.

I reached Aussonce and its Café Des Amis with a shoe full of blood. But seeing the state of me my host to be, a Monsieur Lucien Lund, a monster only in stature, scooped up the whole six foot of me and carried me to a bed in an upstairs room.

I was not, I realised as I took in my surroundings, the only occupant of the room, for at the window stood my friend and erstwhile mid-upper gunner, George Daft!

It was a highly charged reunion, for until this moment I had believed him to be dead, whereas, shepherded by a different set of people he had been in the café for quite a few weeks. It would be many months, however, before we learnt that our navigator had been picked up and become a prisoner of war.

Lucien and his family and friends took solicitous care of us, but Lucien, an active member of the French Resistance, warned us that we could not move on until the Germans finally stopped searching for the airmen missing from our crash. This was very reasonable, but just the same time soon began to drag, especially as the only exercise we were permitted was to walk around the enclosed courtyard of the café.

June 1942 gave way to July, and we really began to press that it was high time we were moved on. Then a pistol-toting individual turned up charging that we were under-cover Germans sniffing out patriots. Things got a bit fraught when we could not answer

German troops guard Allied prisoners after Dieppe, 19 August 1942.

questions on England. As, who was Queen Elizabeth's husband? King George the Sixth, we replied. 'No', the other pounced, 'she had no husband, she was a virgin.' At which first one side then the other saw the funny side of things and showing our identity discs concluded the matter. In retrospect, a ludicrous encounter. Yet neither George nor I had the slightest doubt as to what would have happened had we failed to convince the Resistance of our bona fides.

One thing this Resistance leader insisted upon was that the Allies were to launch a Second Front invasion just days later, on 19 August 1942. We demurred, but were told that two senior German officers had warned the Resistance that their forces were already standing to arms, that in turn the message had been passed to Britain and acknowledged as genuine but that the scheme was to go ahead. And the venue for the unlikely event? Dieppe, he told us.

The Resistance's plan for us, therefore, was to hold us here until the invaders came close, then effect our return. And unlikely as the whole thing seemed we began to get very excited.

Of course, the debacle of Dieppe duly took place and was taken locally for a serious essay at invasion. Exactly what it had been, however, not only puzzled the German High Command, but, I dare venture, speaking with hindsight, not a few of their Allied counterparts.

The news, trumpeted by the German-controlled local press, shattered our hopes. We realised that the badly-shaken Resistance would need time to reassess the situation and make other arrangements for us. Nevertheless, we began berating Lucien and his associates. It is our duty, we declared stridently, to get back to our units and continue bombing the Boche. By delaying our return, we charged they were failing in their own duty as our allies.

And so we stormed and so we strutted. But, in truth, both George and I had long determined that nothing would ever get us into another bomber!

Things settled, but the day came when Lucien appeared, sad-faced, to say that he was to lose us the next morning, that a way forward had finally been found to move us on.

And now that time had come, we found ourselves battling with very mixed emotions. We owed so much to Lucien and his family, yet while there we represented a constant threat. Then again, the world outside the secure café was so hostile. Certainly, there were moist eyes when the door closed behind us.

Our next destination proved to be the Red Cross centre in Reims, our lady guides demanding our promise that we would never reveal the organisation's involvement in our evasion. We gave the promise, and blithely enough. Yet I, for one, doubted that I had it in me to resist the sort of interrogation the Germans would put me through if I were picked up.

We were accommodated in a first floor flat where the artist owner went out of his way to make us welcome not only plying us with food and drink but also allowing us to listen to the BBC on his wireless set. This, however, turned out to be only an overnight stay, for next morning we were taken in tow by a young man who, introducing himself as Henri, told us that he would be accompanying us throughout the next few stages of our journey.

In fact, that day's journey was a walk of just forty minutes – though there seemed to be Germans in every street! – to the house of a couple named Aubin. It soon became clear that Henri had not met them before, but they put all three of us at our ease. It soon became evident too, that they believed in openness. Accordingly, when two of their friends turned up they were at once told who we were. This clearly unsettled Henri, who left shortly afterwards. But perhaps that was by arrangement, for two days later he reappeared, this time to lead us to Dijon, a distance of 120 miles.

Germans on every street.

The journey was made by bus and called for several changes, so that it was late evening before we arrived at the small hotel where we were to stay. First thing next morning, however, we were off again, this time bound for Chagny, on the border of what was variously known as Vichy, Unoccupied, or Free France.

Having left the bus, Henri led us several miles beyond the town, finally turning off along a cart track to reach a cottage. And here a delightful surprise awaited us in the form of a beautiful and vivacious young woman who called herself Blanche and who, we discovered, had already escorted over two dozen evading airmen into Vichy. Her technique, she explained, was to ride her bicycle ahead of the group, stopping at each corner, then dropping a handkerchief if the coast was clear. She warned us that the frontier had no real meaning in the sense of demarcation, that if the Germans patrolling the border spotted us they would cross into Vichy France without a qualm and pull us in. The good thing, she told us, was that their border patrols were too thinly stretched to be all that effective.

As it was, we met no patrols, but just in case, having made our farewells, crossed into Vichy at a run, Henri keeping us going for a good two miles.

Both George and I had assumed that once we were into Unoccupied France the need for vigilance would be over. Henri quickly disabused us.

'No,' he said seriously, 'now we must be particularly careful, for being Vichy France they don't consider themselves to be at war. So though the police won't give you up, they'll certainly imprison you. And who knows when the Germans will choose to take control…'

The next stage took us to Chalon, where the patron of a bar – his palm having been liberally crossed by Henri – proved friendly and furnished us with food and drinks. I have to admit that both George and I tended to let drink loosen our tongues. As a consequence the patron caught on to who and what we were. Just the same, he then offered to put us up, refusing to take any extra money but warning that police patrols routinely called in for a break. The police duly appeared, but having had a drink or two, went on their way.

Next morning, during a thirty-minute wait for the Lyons bus, there was an uncomfortable period after I realised that the three of us were being stonily regarded by a policeman. My heart was in my throat when he finally moved towards us.

'Good morning, gentlemen,' he greeted us. Then he actually winked! 'Good journey, and good luck.' And he walked off.

Lyons turned out to be a thriving place, but the walk to our next haven, a third-floor flat, was so protracted that long before we got there I was in agony from my damaged knee.

Our hosts for the next three days were the Valdants, Jean and his wife, both of whom set out to make us comfortable. We did leave the apartment once, however, Henri announcing that we were to have lunch at a club with, as he put it, some businessmen.

This was surprising enough, but when we were picked up by car, then dropped off at a veritable mansion, we could hardly believe it. Nor did disbelief entirely leave us when we met our hosts, American movie gangsters to a tee!

In fact, they were leading members of the de Gaullist Resistance in the South of France, and were to vet us. Fortunately, we passed muster and enjoyed a meal at which nothing was stinted, the atmosphere becoming so cordial that only later did it once more cross my mind that it was as well for us that they accepted us as genuine evaders.

As it was, at the end of the meal, one of them – he answered to 'Gabriel' – took us into a basement where, by dint of turning a handle, one of several similar machines distributed seemingly unlimited sums of money in various denominations. 'Take it,' Gabriel urged, 'you'll need it for expenses further down the line.' Rather gingerly we took advantage of his offer. Henri and Jean, we noticed, were far less hesitant and quite literally stuffed their pockets.

The next day it was yet another parting of the ways. We were to travel on some 200 miles, to Marseilles, Jean having procured us train tickets the previous evening. He stayed to wave Henri and the two of us off, after which we were taken into the care of the train's conductor, who was, Henri assured us, another trusted member of the organisation.

On reaching Marseilles we once again found ourselves trailing Henri through literally miles of streets arriving thoroughly footsore at our accommodation, a doctor's house: 'Rest that knee,' was his professional advice!

Inside, one of the first people to greet us was an RAF officer who had been shot down only a week before. His welcome aside, though, the atmosphere was far less relaxed than at any of the other 'safe houses' we had sheltered in, the stream of furtive visitors showing it to be primarily a centre for de Gaullist activists. Settling us, Henri took his leave, warning us that it would be a few days before he returned.

It had long intrigued us that Henri had stayed with us over so many stages, and although he never confided in us we later deduced that he was, in fact, either setting up a new escape line or patching rents in an established one.

He duly reappeared, with train tickets for Perpignan, where we arrived without interference. On leaving the train, and concerned over my knee, the towering Pyrenees gave me to think. To my relief, however, Henri set off for the coast, stopping at last at a café where we lingered until darkness fell. Leading the way again, he then walked us for a good distance more before stopping at a darkened building proclaiming itself, Hotel du Tennis. Here, he turned aside from the front entrance and led us down a narrow alley until, having negotiated a locked door, he ushered us into a well-lit cellar. Beckoning us past him, he stood aside, to reveal some fifty upturned faces!

* * *

During the hours we spent in the cellar we were to discover that, among its variegated denizens there were just three Britons; one RAF evader and two soldiers who had been trying to get home since Dunkirk. Most of those present, it transpired, were Jews, this house being the last stage on an escape route that handled all manner of refugees. We got the dampening impression that a previous attempt to get these people away had come to nothing.

Just after midnight, however, the door opened again and after a briefing we were all led onto the sands. We were told to look for two red signal lights. Which I found somewhat ironical. It was full circle. I had 'engineered' my way through the colour-blindness tests to get into aircrew, but red remained the one colour I was unable to make out!

There was no lack of non-defective eyes, however, and not long afterwards a dinghy beached and began to take us off. It belonged, we soon discovered, to the felucca fishing boat *Seawolf* (commander Lucasz), operated by the Polish Naval Mission based in Gibraltar, and acting, in this instance, as part of the protracted refugee-gathering Operation Rosalind. It was 12 October 1942.

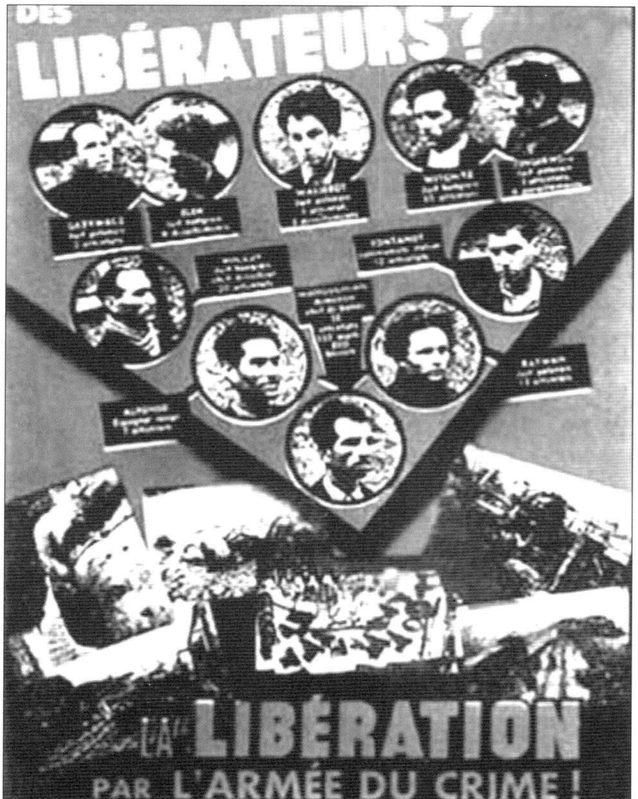

The Resistance are not liberators, but criminals.

Before boarding it was finally time to say farewell to Henri. We tried to express our thanks, but it was impossible to do justice to our feelings. I tried to persuade him to come with us, but he was adamant. His job lay here, he insisted, when he hoped to be able to lead many more evading aircrew to carry on the fight. And so we parted. Henri bound for Occupied France, George and I for Gibraltar, and for Home.

* * *

The felucca Seawolf, *transferring passengers to motor trawler HMS* Tarana *during covert landing operations. (Source, via* Secret Flotillas*, Sir Brooks Richards.)*

I will not detail the onward journey to UK, merely say that when I arrived, unheralded – the official notification signal from Gibraltar having gone astray – it was to shock, but equally to delight, my wife.

The euphoria of my homecoming, may, for a brief space, have taken my mind from all those who had helped make it possible. I can faithfully say, though, that throughout the rest of the war, not least with MI9, I made such helpers my especial concern. After all, records show that 2,803 RAF, and rather more American, airmen evaded with the help of 'ordinary' people in the occupied countries of Europe. The terrible dimension added by post-war historians, however, holds that for every Allied airman who successfully evaded, one civilian helper was executed: *some six thousand, then*!

It was years, of course, before I could begin to try to ascertain the fate of those that had aided George and me. And then it was only with limited success.

That great bear of a man Lucien Lund, I found had been arrested and, though not shot outright, had emerged from a concentration camp as a shadow of his former self, to die within days of returning home. His widow, Susanne, and their children survived, however, and I was able to visit them.

The so-beautiful Blanche was apprehended shortly after we had passed through her section, although her fate is unknown. Jean Valdant and his wife survived and remained in contact for many years. But Henri, our tenacious guide, had vanished into oblivion.

I shall not dwell on my RAF service after my return to Britain, save to say that I served on, was commissioned on 8 December 1943, and saw the RAF Escaping Society into being on 19 June 1946. Having left the Service, I eventually became domiciled in Derbyshire, living in both Hucklow and Bradwell – taking over Bradwell's Bowling Green pub – before moving to Tufa Cottage, in the Via Gellia, at Bonsall, near Matlock.

The general public tends to cast all aircrew in a heroic mould. But it is with no false modesty that I entitle my narrative, *The Ungallant Airman*

'Ungallant'?

Here was an airman, married with children, who had clawed his way into aircrew, deliberately concealing a medical history which must have otherwise barred him had he not so zealously pressurised the board.

An airman, moreover, whose facility with statistics left him in no doubt that his chances of surviving a tour of bomber operations were slender, to say the least.

An airman who, between ops, might bemoan his lot with a fellow sufferer at the bar, yet who never made that guaranteed releasing call either to the squadron office or to the station doctor. A too-imaginative airman moreover – dreadful affliction! – who endured agonies throughout every operational flight and yet more in the sleepless hours after his return; yet one who doggedly climbed aboard the next time his name appeared on the order of battle. And the next ...

An airman who, having been shot down in circumstances of great trauma, might well have taken the easy option and let himself be apprehended. Instead, although overly impatient at times and variously revealing his tense state, he evaded down the length of France, to Spain. What he did not record in his memoir is that he rose to the rank of Wing Commander and that in recognition of both his operational service and his protracted evasion, he was gazetted on 5 February 1943 for the award of the Distinguished Flying Medal.

An ungallant airman? Hardly. Rather, one of the most truly gallant of his gallant peers. Hence the preferred title, *A Truly Gallant Airman.*

The Distinguished Flying Medal (DFM).

Signal recommending the Distinguished Flying Medal

```
Immediate. D.G. Southwell 1255623 Sergt 35 Sqd:
Sorties 8, Flying hours 37.21 W.Op/AG. Sergeant
Southwell was the WOP/AG in an aircraft which took
off from Linton-on-Ouse at 22.30 Hrs on 19/5/42, to
bomb Mannheim. Prior to reaching the target, they
were shot down and Sergt Southwell was injured when
landing. With great courage and determination, he
evaded capture and eventually arrived back in this
country. I recommend the award of the D.F.M.
```

(London Gazette *5/2/1943; Records Office reference Air2/4937.)*

8

Relieving Fortress Malta

Flying Officer Dennis Cocke
wireless operator/air gunner

In June 1940 I was working as a photographer in the Public Record Office but the moment I was old enough I enlisted in the RAF Volunteer Reserve. Once called forward, I reported to Uxbridge and having applied for aircrew duties, was given a medical and accepted for training in the dual role of wireless operator/air gunner (WOp/AG).

The first training stage was carried out at the Initial Training Wing at Blackpool where we did our general service training and, among other ground subjects, began to learn morse. Next came a move to No. 2 Wireless School at Yatesbury, in Wiltshire, where we were instructed in radio theory and basic navigation. At the end of the course, having reached the required speed at morse, we proudly found ourselves designated aircraftmen class two, aircrew under training (AC2, Aircrew U/T), and stitched the wireless flash onto our right sleeves.

Next came the gunnery training which I began in March 1941 at No. 1 Central Gunnery School at Warmwell in Dorset, and completed in December 1941 at Castle Kennedy in Ayrshire.

After that came No. 3 Radio School at Prestwick, where we were introduced to the Air-to-Surface-Vessel radar (ASV) which gave us a maplike display of the earth's surface, highlighting the coastlines and showing any vessels as bright spots, or blips. For security it was referred to as the 'Special Installation' or SI.

After Prestwick came No. 8 Bombing and Gunnery School at Evanton, on the Cromarty Firth, which I passed out from on 16 February 1942 and so became a sergeant, qualified to wear the coveted AG (air gunner) brevet on my left breast.

Finally, together with other newly-qualified aircrew, I reported to RAF Cranwell which housed, among its lodger concerns, No. 3 (Coastal) Operational Training Unit (OTU), then equipped with Wellingtons.

Here, the moment we had finished taking around our 'arrival' chits, we were directed

The crew: top left: *Sergeant Jim Howard, RNZAF, co-pilot;* top right: *Sergeant John Davey, rear gunner.* Bottom, left to right: *Sergeant Jim Foster, ASV (or SI) operator; Pilot Officer Brian Misslebrook, navigator/bomb aimer; Sergeant Dennis Cooke, wireless operator/air gunner; Pilot Officer Vivien Hodnett, captain.*

to mix and mingle and so sort ourselves into crews. A somewhat daunting procedure but one which seemed to work, so that within a short time I found myself a member of a six-man crew.

As formed, this comprised: Pilot Officer Vivien Hodnett, captain; Sergeant Jim Howard, Royal New Zealand Air Force, co-pilot; Pilot Officer Brian Misslebrook, navigator/bomb aimer; me, Sergeant Dennis Cooke, wireless operator/air gunner; Sergeant Jim Foster, ASV (or SI) operator; and Sergeant John Davey, rear gunner.

Brian, the navigator, was a Balkan-Sobranie, pipe-smoking barrister and suspiciously grey-haired, for all that he swore he was just thirty-one. John, in the rear turret, had worked for the Co-op in Port Glasgow and was, of course, 'Jock'. Jim Foster's family owned a fish and chip shop in Bramley, Leeds, so that on one occasion when a couple of the crew passed through Leeds on leave they found Jim officiating behind the counter. 'The bugger,' they complained when they came back, 'he made us pay!' The captain, Viv – well, I can't really say what he did ... if he'd done anything by then. Possibly he hadn't yet taken up an occupation. He was a grammar school type, and had a very pleasant mother, I remember. After the war, when he married his cousin I stood in as her godfather, so what relation that made Viv to me, I cannot say! And Jim Howard was a New Zealander who, whatever he had been doing before the war, made a career in flying domestic routes when he returned home. We were all so young!

Once crewed up, and gelling swiftly as we went along, we began to learn the art of Coastal Command warfare, overflying land and sea in a series of exercises in Vickers Wellington Mk.8s, the version known as the 'Stickleback' because of the four sticking-up, dorsal-mounted (or top-of-the-fuselage) aerials of the Mk.2 ASV equipment.

During these flights I would receive weather information, take navigational bearings, and assist the SI operator in locating targets and obtaining pinpoints. Where communications were concerned, however, ordinary training was behind us and on these operationally-oriented sorties it was largely a case of maintaining a listening-only watch. Any messages we did transmit were encrypted beforehand using a device known as the pyscho, the operator's plain language being converted according to a daily-changed code.

At the end of this final course, with the crew now operationally ready, we found ourselves posted to the Middle East, initially to No. 221 Squadron, at that time operating from Landing Ground No. 89 in the Egyptian Desert. So it was that on 6 June 1942 we left Portreath, in Cornwall, and routed out via Gibraltar and Malta to Cairo, entraining then to Alexandria before being taken by lorry to join the squadron.

We arrived just as an urgent appeal for more Wellingtons was received from Headquarters Malta. In response, our crew was among those detached, at the double,

A sea-hugging Coastal Command Wellington Mk.8 with Air-to-Surface-Vessel (ASV) Mk.2 radar aerials.

so to speak, to become the Special Duties Flight of Malta's resident No. 69 Squadron, at that time carrying out anti-shipping strikes from the besieged and bomb-battered island.

Landing at Malta's main airfield, Luqa, in April 1942 we at once began a life of marauding against enemy shipping at night and being bombed by day-flying Axis (German and Italian) aircraft while we tried to rest.

The Italians had first raided Malta nearly two years before, on 11 June 1940, and since the Germans had become involved there had been multiple raids every day. When we arrived, therefore, the besieged island had long been on desperately short rations, indeed an abiding memory of my stay there is of always being both tired out and hungry. The truth was, though, that desperate as the food shortage was, the most pressing need was for aviation fuel, for without air cover the island was bound to fall.

Hopes for Malta's continued resistance were raised early in June 1942 when two convoys, codenamed Operation Vigorous (from Haifa and Port Said) and Operation Harpoon (from Gibraltar), were dispatched simultaneously. That hope was shattered when both were virtually annihilated, just two transports reaching Valetta Harbour.

By August 1942, consequently, with vital stocks at absolute rock bottom, Malta's High Command was on tenterhooks as it awaited the arrival of the surviving ships from Operation Pedestal, a supply convoy of fourteen merchant vessels escorted by forty-

August 1942, Malta, and a day's rations ...

Operation Pedestal, HMS Kenya *(adopted by Derby) under air attack.*

four warships which had suffered incessant sea and air attacks since leaving Gibraltar.

On 11 August 1942 a grievous loss was sustained when HMS *Eagle*, one of the four aircraft carriers in support, was sunk by a submarine. Then, the very next day, with the depleted convoy so near its goal, Headquarters was electrified by a photo-reconnaissance report that a significant force of Italian warships was heading south to intercept it. As it was imperative that the enemy fleet was positively located, three of our Wellingtons were detailed to find them and monitor their progress.

Two of the aircraft got airborne on time but ours was delayed owing to a radar fault. We eventually became serviceable, though, and got airborne at 0135 hours on 13 August 1942 when, on opening up a listening watch with HQ Malta, I found that signals traffic – and Italian interference – was unusually heavy.

Such signals interference put our defences to a great deal of extra trouble. Fortunately, we had what might be called a secret weapon in the form of a Canadian Jew – his name slips my mind – who had developed a facility with radio countermeasures. As a ground signals officer he had invented some form of equipment which, from what we could make of it, involved him swiping a rheostat over the interference and re-setting our own frequencies clear of it. He was not aircrew but in developing his device he flew so often that Air Vice Marshal Sir Keith Park, who had come to the Middle East after his triumphs in the Battle of Britain, conferred the Distinguished Flying Cross upon him.

As a personal aside, I was so impressed with this technical wizard that some time later, when I was at Turnberry, I penned an outline account of his activities and submitted it for publication. Only to be carpeted and awarded a reprimand for breaching security regulations!

But back then, having set off from Malta, we avoided the worst of the interference, duly reached the search area and commenced our pattern. And successfully so, for at about 0330 hours Jim Foster, on the ASV, detected the hostile fleet. We homed to a safe distance, keeping the ships in sight as our navigator/bomb aimer, Brian Misselbrook, dropped two flares. Using these he was able to obtain the drift which, in turn, allowed him to calculate the speed and direction of the vessels, information which he then passed to me for sending off as an encoded sighting signal.

And what invigorating information it was! For at briefing we had been told that the Italian fleet was heading southwards on an attack heading, whereas our observations showed that it was now on a northerly heading and steaming directly away from the convoy!

What had already taken us aback while flying towards the search area had been to hear messages addressed to our other two aircraft, already on station, and transmitted, of all things, in plain language. Messages, at that, which mystified us. One of them, which I logged at 0319 hours just before we had located and begun shadowing our quarry, asked for an updated position for the Italian fleet 'for the guidance of the Liberators'. Yet we knew full well that none of these heavy bombers was engaged. But then, at 0356 hours, I received a signal directly addressed to our aircraft, instructing us to 'attack the cruisers then return', again in plain language. '*Then return* ...' Yes!

It seemed more than a bit suicidal, a lone Wellington being directed to attack a whole fleet of capital ships, but orders were orders. So we duly set up an attack pattern and dropped all eight of our 250 pound bombs in a single stick. Suicidal indeed, for as if Brian's 'Bombs gone!' command had been a signal the sky around us instantly filled with flak, so that for some time Viv had all his work cut out to fly us clear.

Once we were on course for Luqa, however, Brian passed me an enhanced sighting

The vital oil tanker SS Ohio *enters Valletta harbour on 15 August 1942*

signal confirming that the hostile force was indeed heading northwards and away from the convoy. Then, when we had pulled well clear, and with John Davey in the rear turret keeping a good lookout for fighters, Jim Howard, our co-pilot, spelled Viv at the controls, handing over again for the landing at just before 0600 hours.

Having passed the aircraft over to the groundcrew we had great difficulty in staying awake throughout an unusually detailed debriefing. When we got to our beds, however, we slept the sleep of the just, never doubting that it been the timely and aggressive action of our own flight's three Wellingtons that had persuaded the Italian battle fleet to turn for home.

It was a nice conceit. But eventually we learnt quite a bit more about Operation Pedestal and the measures taken to ensure that as many of its components as possible received protection. Not least, that of the fourteen merchant ships bringing the vital supplies, only four had so far survived. In fact, the very next night we were patrolling for nearly eight hours as part of the air shield for the fifth survivor, the immensely important but now crippled tanker SS *Ohio* (at that time the largest tanker in the world) as it limped its way towards Malta to deliver its crucial cargo of aviation fuel.

All that we learnt while the enterprise was ongoing. In time, though, there was also a certain amount of enlightenment for the mystifyingly uncoded signals we had received. It emerged that Headquarters Malta had deliberately transmitted in plain language – on all signals networks – to ensure that the Axis instantly got the message that Allied heavy bombers were actually on their way. Italian naval records show that they became aware of the threat at about midnight. As their German allies had refused from the outset to furnish them with air cover for the foray, it was only politic that they should order their ships to turn about and return to port.

Headquarters Malta, of course, had sent out the lure, but perforce blindly and knowing that only time would tell whether the enemy had taken the bait, proof of this being that between 0300 and 0400 hours HQ were still playing 'the Liberator game' in messages to us. So our signal telling them that the Italians were now heading north was of critical moment. Not, perhaps, the feather we had initially stuck in our caps on getting to bed but one well worth crowing under nonetheless.

At debriefing that night, then, we may not have known the whole picture, but I evidently felt that the operation had been of more than normal significance because I went as far as removing the relevant pages from my wireless telegraphy log and stowing them with my belongings! Heinous for any wireless operator! Yet I was clearly acting on the side of the angels – albeit inadvertently – for a full fifty-five years later I was contacted by Admiral of the Fleet Lord Lewin, an erstwhile member of the Operation Pedestal support fleet, who had read an article I had written and urged me to be 'very public spirited', so persuading me to deposit the purloined pages with the Imperial War Museum.

The *Ohio* had brought in the vital supply of aviation fuel, and so Malta's fight was able to continue: it really had been that close! Of course, with adequate supplies of fuel to hand there was to be no cessation from the Wellington detachment's routine of troglodytic days and sea-sweeping nights; the very reverse, in fact. Nor was life getting any less stressful for our particular crew.

We were all suffering from the dual strains of flying anti-shipping strikes against heavily armed and violently aggressive vessels, then of incessantly being bombed when we were trying to rest on the ground. To make matters worse we had nothing but near-starvation rations with which to sustain our flagging endurance. Among the crew, however, a more insidious concern had surfaced, for we had begun to feel that our two pilots were becoming more rattled than the rest of us, even sheering aside from targets. This was neither good, nor productive, for only by pressing home our attacks and successfully flying reckonable sorties could we hope to earn the respite a completed tour of thirty operations would bring us.

It was clear, however, that the squadron bosses had become similarly concerned, for our co-pilot, Jim Howard, was taken off flying and left the island to be rested. Then, on 13 October 1942, the commanding officer flew with us as captain, detailing Viv to act as second pilot, repeating the monitoring exercise a few days later. Indeed, on that occasion we actually illuminated a stationary U-boat, so facilitating an attack!

Having assessed Viv during these two flights the CO evidently considered that he had settled sufficiently, for on 16 October 1942 Viv resumed command with a Flight Sergeant Rowe as his second pilot. That first trip, however, was hardly a fair test of Viv's supposedly renewed mettle, for having got airborne we ran into one of the Med's more virulent electrical storms and after a fruitless two hours he understandably abandoned the sortie. On a subsequent trip, though, in perfect weather, he decided that the elevator was acting up and aborted the trip. Another non-op!

Our next flight of note took place on 28 October 1942, yet another potentially fraught anti-shipping strike. An hour out, however, and some time before reaching the target area, Viv advised that the port engine was losing power, at which he ordered the bombs to be jettisoned and warned us to prepare to ditch.

As we busied ourselves about our pre-ditching duties – Brian jettisoning the bombs and calculating a position for my distress signal – Viv and the second pilot, a Flight Sergeant Fowler, talked the situation over. I remember them discussing whether or not to stop the engine and feather the propeller: that is, to turn the blades edge-on to the airflow to minimise drag. I can only conclude, though, that I was so busy tuning my set that the decision they came to did not register. Yet it must have concerned me at the time, for although our advanced mark of machine did have propellers that could be feathered it was no happier on one engine than any other Wellington, and there was an awful lot of Mediterranean between us and the island.

So it was that I came to send off my first actual distress message, and was gratified to get an immediate acknowledgement from Malta. As it transpired, Viv, monitored throughout – cajoled, perhaps – by Flight Sergeant Fowler, kept the aircraft in the air and on arrival positioned for a straight-in approach to Luqa.

Only here he gave himself a problem, for by coming straight in off the sea he had picked up none of the spatial references that flying a circuit of the airfield might have given him. Finding himself too high, therefore, he was then faced with carrying out an overshoot and, once past the palely-shining runway, penetrating an inky-blackness that would have called for at least some reliance on instruments. When he found himself too high on his second approach and was forced to overshoot again, he must have been badly rattled. Even more so if he was conscious – as any captain would be – that his crew had become, to say the least, disaffected. Hardly surprising then that his third attempt was nothing short of disastrous.

It happened that, having successfully done my bit at the wireless set, I was spelling John Davey in the rear turret for the landing. I duly watched, horrified, as I saw the whole length of the runway disappear behind me and then, after a few moments of grinding and bumping, realised that we had crashed. In fact, into one of Malta's ubiquitous quarries. The aircraft was a write-off but nobody on board was seriously hurt.

With regard to the suspect port engine, next day I secured a photograph of the crash, which shows both props unfeathered: so either the pilots decided to feather and then

Our aircraft looking sad, finally down after two overshoots.

to restart the engine for the approach, or they had kept both engines going throughout. Whichever way it was handled, over-tired Viv soon followed in Jim Howard's train and left the island.

As replacements we got two Australian flight-sergeant pilots, Swin Hansen, and Cameron, whose first name now escapes me.

Shipping strikes continued, as did the losses. When, on 20 November 1942, four cargo ships docked successfully – after which living conditions improved and enemy bombing slackened – we, as a crew, were still living on the edge of our nerves; more particularly as we inched closer to completing our quota of operational sorties.

We actually reached our thirtieth on the evening of 24 November 1942 when we took off on yet another shipping strike. Having located the enemy vessels Swin immediately commenced an attack. The moment the bombs had gone, however, heavy and very accurate flak forced him to take the most extreme evasive action, abruptly pushing the nose down towards the sea. At which point the port engine chose to cut!

As we hurriedly prepared to take up ditching stations I transmitted my second-ever distress call but this time, being so low – barely skimming the waves – with little hope of its being received. Just moments later, however, and I never did find out how they managed it, the dead engine burst into life again and Swin was able to lift us clear.

As we gained height I was to be gratified twice-over, first by our reprieve, and secondly by discovering that my tuning had been accurate and that the SOS had, in fact, got through, albeit to a distant station, for I heard a Cairo-based radio operator relaying it to Malta.

Eleven hours and twenty minutes that final op took us. Four days later, and safely tour-ex, we saw Malta finally fade into the distance behind us. For all that we felt for the gallant populace – the George Cross the island was collectively awarded was so well deserved – how glad we were to wave them farewell!

With our tour completed we were due a rest from operations. Our pilots and our navigator were flown back to the UK but we three wireless operators were given a temporary posting to the Aircraft Delivery Unit at Cairo. As it turned out, this lasted until March 1943, after which we were transported from Freetown, Sierra Leone, to Liverpool in SS *Mauritania*.

The allotted seven days of leave fairly flashed past, after which I discovered that my 'rest' posting required me to fly as a wireless operator instructor at No. 1 Torpedo Training Unit at Turnberry, Ayrshire. I was very well aware, however, of the accident rate at this unit My unease was shared by Eric Cameron, a Canadian friend from Malta's No. 69 Squadron who had been similarly posted in. He was equally appalled that we might be uselessly killed while doing nothing productive.

'We'd be safer on a squadron. What d'ya say we go back to ops?' he proposed.

My response, 'I can't stand all this bullshit,' owed more to my dislike of Training Command than to the casualty figures. But acting on our misgivings we immediately applied for a transfer back to operational flying and a second tour.

Approval came through gratifyingly quickly. Only to our dismay, although we were posted to another operational squadron within Coastal Command, it was to No. 489 Squadron, Royal New Zealand Air Force. For this unit was stationed at Wick, in Caithness, and was still operating antiquated Hampden torpedo bombers: a case of out of the frying pan, and with a vengeance! The only good thing, we mutually decided, was that we had not been directed towards Bomber Command!

Just the same, we fared rather better than we might have expected, for the commander of 'A' Flight was looking for a new crew and, impressed that we had flown on torpedo operations against Axis shipping in the Med, he immediately took us on.

Such, then, was Flight Lieutenant Stanley William Kellow, DFC, a Londoner, somewhat older than the rest of us, and a man who immediately engendered respect.

... coded message for base.

Our navigator was a young flying officer – in this case it is his surname that escapes me, although we knew him as Cyril. As for Eric and me, now both flight sergeants, Eric habitually took his station in the twin-Vickers-equipped top turret while I felt more useful operating the Marconi T1154/R1155 transmitter/receiver and keeping an eye on the caged pigeon we would launch if the wireless equipment let us down. And so we settled in with a series of navigational exercises.

Stan's piloting im-

The long outmoded Handley Page Hampden

pressed us from the start, but we were not in the least enamoured of the veteran Hampden, an aircraft which had been 'let go' by Bomber Command as far back as late 1942. As a type it was remarkable among British aircraft in having its occupants packed towards the front of the three-foot wide fuselage. Despite the proximity, however, there was virtually no access to any other crew member; no chance, then, of benefiting from the gregarious support which we understood the packed-together German bomber crews took heart from. Certainly, my view of all our Hampden operations was restricted to what I could see through a gun hatch on the port side.

The squadron's task had originally been to search out submarines, but by the time we arrived it had switched to what were known as 'Torpedo Rovers', operations in which a single aircraft would hunt out and attack enemy shipping in and around the Norwegian ports and the North Sea.

For us, the first of these sorties took place on 14 September 1943, except that the weather was almost unworkable so that, lacking the ASV – the surface mapping radar – Eric and I had become accustomed to, and although we battled against the weather for nearly four hours, we found nothing.

What we soon discovered, however, following that first op of our second tour, was why Stan's New Zealander colleagues had bestowed upon him the press-on nickname of 'Ship Buster', for as sortie followed sortie it became evident that he had a knack of sniffing out enemy ships, particularly when Rovers were mounted at dawn or dusk and in foul-weather conditions when a detected enemy might be momentarily caught off guard.

A month into our tour, in October 1943, the squadron moved to Leuchars to cover an increase in enemy shipping using the Skagerrack sea channel to the north of

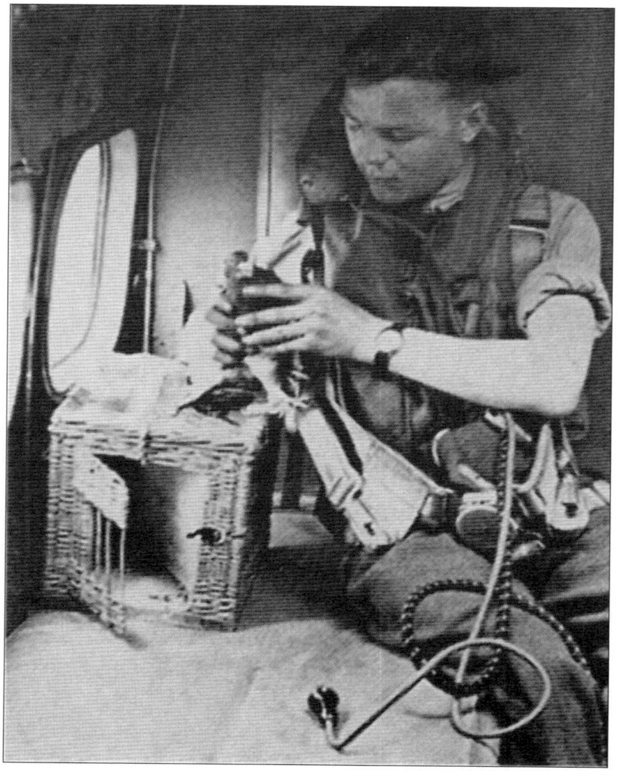

Readying carrier pigeons for communications duty.

Denmark. One of our flights, on 26 October 1943, was rather more typical of the Rovers than the first had been although, as it transpired, it was to be our last Hampden op.

Having crossed the North Sea we made a landfall to the south of Stavanger, after which Stan – by this time *Squadron Leader* Stan Kellow – turned further south down the coast, hugging the rock-strewn ground. Looking out of my side hatch all I could see was a continuous series of flashes, seemingly innocuous but betokening potentially lethal anti-aircraft fire just the same. Nobody spoke until, after what seemed like an endless period of boulder-scraping, Stan rapped, 'Stand-by, crew, target dead ahead, I'm going straight in.' What he had discovered, it rapidly became clear, was a whole cluster of enemy vessels in a sheltered anchorage!

As he turned seawards to commence the attack I could see the ground zipping by just inches below until, reaching a headland, he pushed downwards towards the water. As the nose dropped I was lifted off my feet, then instants later, flattened to the floor by the 'g' force as he levelled the Hampden out. I heard the bomb doors open, and moments later, felt the machine surge upwards as the torpedo dropped away.

'Get a picture, Eric,' Stan yelled, even as flak began to buffet the sky around us. I had time to see red-cored, brownish-black puffs of smoke fill my vantage point before, as Stan took what evasive action he could at that level, what felt like a monster hand pressed me to the floor once more. Nor was I the only g-force casualty, for an ammunition drum crashed down beside me, as did the pigeon's metal cage, so that as Stan continued to turn and twist us clear I, the communications expert, found my true vocation in trying to placate our feathered communicator.

Eventually things smoothed out and I began to breathe again. Moments later, when Stan did a crew check Eric responded at once, as I did, reporting my own continued wellbeing: I hardly felt I could legitimately speak for the pigeon. However, when there was no answer from Cyril, I clambered down and peering forwards, could just see him, leant unmoving across his chart table in the nose. I shouted but there was no response, so fearing the worst I stretched out my leg – the only way to reach him – and kicked his foot. Startled, he looked around, realised at once that his intercom plug had become disconnected during Stan's gyrations, reconnected it and hastily checked in. He too, had come to no harm.

Satisfied that we were all fit and well, Stan returned to the business in hand. 'Send a sighting report,' he ordered. 'Two MVs [motor vessels] and one destroyer. Position, probably Egersund.'

'It *was* Egersund', confirmed Cyril, and moments later passed me a coded message for base.

Back at Leuchars – with a relieved pigeon safe in its loft – a disappointment lay in store. Eric's photograph showed absolutely no evidence of damage! Not even the hint of an explosion. Stan was confident that he had released the torpedo at the correct range, between four and five hundred yards, but from the testimony of the photograph he could only assume that by the time the weapon reached the target it had still not lifted to its pre-set running depth and had, therefore, passed harmlessly beneath the vessel's keel.

Not the best of ways to finish our time together but it turned out that ours had been the last Hampden to go into action and to return safely. And with that niche in aviation history we had to be content. For just days after that the squadron was re-equipped with Beaufighters and I was redundant, the type having no position for a wireless operator/air gunner.

A new posting soon arrived, still within Coastal Command but to No. 524 Squadron at Davidstow Moor in Cornwall. Before leaving Leuchars, however, I had been recommended for a commission and was duly gazetted as a pilot officer in November 1944.

My new squadron were operating Wellingtons in the maritime reconnaissance role, the task being to locate German torpedo boats, and then summon other units to attack them. These E-boats, as we called them – more properly Schnellboot (S-boot), or 'fast craft' – were much larger than our equivalent vessels and having a range of some 700 miles were a constant hazard to our shipping.

As with all over-sea patrols these sweeps could be both boring and uneventful. Some stand out, like the one we did covering the area from Cherbourg to the Channel Islands when, off Alderney, we were coned by searchlights, an experience which instantly drove

D-Day – just part of the invasion fleet ...

away any tendency towards lethargy.

Another of these anti-E-boat sweeps which lives in the memory was the one we carried out on the night of 5 June 1944. We got airborne at 2300 hours, flew to Brest, then quartered the English Channel until it was time to turn for home. At, I fancy, something like 0500 hours, we had just set course to leave the patrol area when suddenly both pilot and nav burst out, '*Christ, it's started*!' At which the rest of us peered down and saw hundreds upon hundreds of white wakes arrowing through the mist and steadily moving towards the enemy-occupied coast. The long-awaited Second Front had begun! It was D-Day! The Invasion! And Eisenhower had omitted to tell us!

Another incident during our stay at Davidstow Moor was rather more sobering. We had only just got airborne on a long patrol when we received a bad-weather recall. Fog was always a problem on Davidstow Moor and it was clear that the met people expected so rapid a deterioration to last for some time. Indeed, it was so fast that before we could commence our approach the visibility fell to zero and we were ordered to divert to Dunkeswell, near Honiton, regardless of our fuel state. This meant, effectively, that with the bomb load and virtually our full patrolling fuel, we were pushing the safe all-up-weight for landing. Needless to say, perhaps, we put down somewhat gingerly.

At that time Dunkeswell was being used by the United States Navy as a Liberator base. On this occasion several RAF aircraft had already found refuge there. So, having parked next to another of our squadron's Wellingtons, we disembarked, to find ourselves made much of by the Americans.

Next morning orders came for all the Wellingtons which had diverted there to scrub their ops and return to base directly. We prepared to get under way but then received orders from the American air controller to defuel to an acceptable level before attempting to get airborne. Clearly they had no intention of hazarding their own aircraft by one of ours failing to manage what they feared was an unnecessarily heavily-laden take-off!

The rest of the crew sat down to wait on a bunker wall until at length an American naval rating arrived with an empty fuel bowser. As the rating began unrolling his hose the skipper took his position on the wing, ready to assist. For my part I walked some way off and began to watch the Liberators getting airborne. A moment later, as it seemed, my attention was caught by a muffled, 'Whumpf!' At which I spun about. To see our Wellington in flames!

It transpired that the rating had found that the American hose connector was not compatible with ours. Whether his attempts to jam the nozzle into place had caused a spark, who knows! But the whole thing had gone up on the instant.

The skipper jumped to the ground and without checking his pace, dived head first to join the rest of the crew, now sheltering behind the bunker. I was all set to follow suit. But then I realised that the rating, smothered from head to foot in flames, was staggering my way. I had no option, therefore, but to run towards him, although ammunition was already going off. As we closed, so he fell writhing to the ground. I felt so utterly helpless! Yet I had to do something, so in desperation I began to tear free what clothing would come away, beating out the flames with my hands.

A truck pulled up some distance away, the driver yelling out, 'Any bombs on board?' When I yelled back, 'A full load,' he refused to come any closer. Another rating, though, jumped down, took in the state of the burnt man and asked if I could get him to the truck. By now I'd beaten out the flames but I was horrified to see how the sufferer's skin was peeling back. Somehow, I managed a fireman's lift, and together the two of us bundled the casualty into the truck which rushed him off to the base hospital.

Still somewhat dazed I made my way towards the bunker. 'Keep down,' the rest were yelling as I fell over the bank. And so I did. Just as well, for at that moment the bombs began to go off, one after the other. Fortunately the blasts went skywards, so nobody else was hurt, but the explosions finished off the Wellington beside ours as well. 'You're a bloody hero, Cooke,' one of the air gunners said feelingly.

I certainly did not feel heroic. For a start I was too shocked, and at the same time in too much pain: each of my palms was one huge blister, with another on every joint of my fingers. After a while the Americans dressed my burns, putting on a salve which gradually – very gradually – began to ease things.

A Wellington was dispatched from Davidstow Moor to collect the two dispossessed crews, and on our return we were given seven days' leave. My mother was suitably impressed by my burnt palms but I was left with a nightmare vision of the rating running towards me, a human torch; a nightmare which still visits me on occasion to this day.

Some weeks after the incident, and well after my leave, I happened to be in the vicinity of the orderly room when a clerk beckoned me over: 'There's something for you. Been here quite some time.' And he handed me an envelope.

Opening it – my hands had long regained their function by then – I found that it was a Commendation for Bravery issued and signed by 'William H. Hamilton, Commander of Fleet Air Wing Seven, Air Force, US Navy', for saving the life of 'Robert T. McDaniel, Aviation Machinist Mate 3rd Class, and in doing so sustaining first-degree burns on both your own hands'.

At the time, torn between embarrassment, confusion and perhaps something of guilt for having been able to do so little for the man, I folded the paper and pushed it into my battledress pocket, figuratively pushing it even further from my mind. Only many years later was I able to view the incident – in waking hours, at least – with any sort of equanimity, and to appreciate the honour our Allies had done me.

It transpired that the rating had suffered sixty-five per cent burns. I only learnt that long after the war when I contacted the lady proprietor of what had then become Dunkeswell Aviation Museum who told me that Mr McDaniel, the former rating, had visited not that long before and had actually shown her the scars on his legs!

Dennis Cooke in 2009

In mid 1944 the squadron moved to Norfolk to do the same anti-E-boat duty, but this time off the East Coast, operating variously from Docking, Bircham Newton and Langham. So it was that by the end of hostilities I had completed my second tour, leaving me free to apply for a transfer to Transport Command.

The application was approved, and brought a posting to the Far East which saw me installed as signals officer at No. 8 Staging Post at Mingaladon, Rangoon, in Burma. Here, my duties lay in providing dependable signals information to crews routing through the theatre. It proved to be both a responsible and a time-consuming job and one that kept me busy until my demobilisation came through in 1946.

Looking back, of our old Hampden crew, Eric Cameron survived the war, returned to Canada and stayed in contact, until he died in January 2008. Stan Kellow, however, had been killed in a training accident at Langham on 5 June 1944.

More happily, I met up with Vivien Hodnett quite soon after the war, and, as I have said, became god-father to his bride! Then again, Jim Howard, who had returned to New Zealand, saw an article of mine in 2007, contacted me for the first time in sixty years and has remained in contact as this is written, in late 2010.

As for me, having left the Service I entered the teaching profession, eventually retiring after a career spanning thirty-eight years.

Uncomfortable as my Malta sojourn was, I have always retained a lively interest in what has for so long now been known as the George Cross Island. Indeed in December 2007 the magazine *Aeroplane* published an article – the one Jim saw in New Zealand – on my experiences during the island's ordeal. Before that, though, I had published a book, *Malta Invincible*, the proceeds of which I used to raise funds for the Malta Aviation Museum Foundation. I was highly gratified, therefore, when, as a consequence, the Honorary Citizenship of Valletta was bestowed upon me. Indeed, more than gratified, for the distinction brought me into direct fellowship with those other recipients, the dwindling band of gallant survivors of the so-timely convoy that, as Operation Pedestal, had succoured Malta in her hour of greatest need

Strange to say, though, I have not been back to the island since. Too many memories, perhaps. So for me, Malta lives eternally in the mix of admiration and relief I felt as it finally disappeared behind us back in late November 1942. Gallant little Malta!

Malta under air bombardment, 1942.

9

The Secret

Flight Sergeant Geoffrey Appleyard, DFM
pilot

Sergeant James Douglas (Terry) Davie
rear gunner

Most of the narratives in this book are related by crew members who count themselves lucky to have survived operational flying. Necessarily, this account, a mere fragment from the lives from one particular crew, comes from friends of the young airmen involved.

The only too prophetic 'secret' of the title, imparted by Sergeant James Douglas (Terry) Davie in 1942, was revealed by Mrs Edith Houghton, née Borley, in response to a *Glossop Advertiser* appeal for remembrances of wartime aircrew. Subsequent researches led to Mrs Kathleen Davies (née Neal), a wartime friend of Flight Sergeant Geoffrey Appleyard, DFM. Mrs Davies was able to furnish the complementary story.

The recorded facts are that on 27 July 1942, at 0010 hours, Lancaster R5683 of No. 106 Squadron took off from RAF Coningsby, ten miles north-west of Boston, Lincolnshire, to raid Duisberg. Just minutes later the aircraft came to pieces in the air then crashed and exploded in flames onto the marshy flats of the North Sea coast, four miles east-north-east of Boston. All the crew died, including the rear gunner who had managed to bale out before impact.

Mrs Kathleen Davies (née Neal) recalled:
At that time I lived at Benington, some four miles from Boston and about a mile from where the aircraft crashed. I would have to say now that I knew Geoff Appleyard well, my only rival being his love of flying and his pride in his Lancaster and his crew. Indeed, we were so close that whenever he knew an operation was pending, and before calls

from the station were blocked for security, he would phone me. His excitement would come bubbling through and at some stage he would use the phrase, 'I'm happy', which was our private code meaning that something was on.

Then, some hours later, I would hear the planes going over. In fact, starting from shortly after we met, he would bring his Lancaster low over the house, engines roaring, so that I always knew that he was among them. Then, the moment he could, he would phone to say he was back.

Leading Wren Kathleen Neal, 1943.

Geoff and his crew were great fun and would often stay in my parent's house, all seven of them crammed into our spare bedroom. After my sister Joan and I raided the cupboard for drinks, Geoff concocted a cocktail he called 'Kath's Folly' in my honour. With all of us being around twenty years old we were so happy and carefree!

We'd make snacks at all hours and one time Geoff borrowed my pink apron when he cooked us egg and chips. Then, as it had protected him from the hot fat, he decided it would be a good thing to wear when flying on operations. So he did, and he would have been wearing it that last night. For they all had their mascots, one of the crew carrying – wearing, conceivably – his girl's brassiere!

On the night Geoff died I had not yet closed the curtains after his chimney-shaking farewell overflight, so I saw the horrid red glare out towards the North Sea the moment it started, then heard the noise of the explosions. My mind was in turmoil, for I knew only too well that although there were hundreds of aero-engines overhead still, his aircraft was the one that had crashed.

I dressed quickly, found that my parents had done the same, and all of us went to the scene; to find an inferno. There was nothing we could do, and although it took some time to ascertain that it had indeed been Geoff's aircraft I was never in any real doubt, for all that I tried to hold on to hope. It was a slight comfort, even then, to know that Geoff and his crew would have had no time to feel anything, for that became clear the moment we saw how tiny an area the burning wreckage covered. Then, later still, friends from other crews were able to tell us what few details the investigators had discovered, the court of inquiry ruling that there had been a mechanical failure.

Yet it has always saddened me to think that some mere mechanical failure could have brought such an experienced crew to an end like that when they had been

An inferno …

through so much together: they were, after all, well over halfway into their tour of bombing operations. What made it even more poignant that it was a technical fault was to recall that they, in common with all the fliers we knew, quite literally swore by their groundcrews.

We had many RAF friends at Coningsby, lads who would teach us to dance, and to skate at the Gliderdome, and even after the crash several of them used to fly low over our house during air tests and training. In fact, when they were setting off on raids, some would come down and waggle their wings in salute, just as Geoff used to.

There was such comradeship, and friendship of the sort one would never meet today. On one occasion I was expecting an air-gunner friend to take me to something he knew I especially wanted to see, when another turned up. His friend had not, as he put it, 'made it', but under a pact arranged before the op, he had come in his stead so that I would not be disappointed.

But they were all such lovely lads. Only so many were shot down, and killed. Even then, some survived as prisoners of war. In which case we sent parcels to their various prison camps.

As it happened, it was not the first time I had sent and received letters from Germany because before the war I had corresponded with a pen friend who was a Hitler Youth

Five of the seven crew: Flight Sergeant Montague Darvill, DFM, observer (navigator); Pilot Officer Ray Branton Smith, Royal Canadian Air Force, air bomber (bomb aimer); Flight Sergeant Geoffrey Appleyard, DFM, captain, in pinnie; Sergeant James Douglas (Terry) Davie, rear gunner; Sergeant James William Grimwade, Royal Australian Air Force, wireless operator/air gunner.

leader – being naïve I had thought that compared to a patrol leader in our Boy Scouts. Because of that, though, I was able to send some of his picture postcards of German cities and the like to the Air Ministry's Intelligence Department, a patriotic measure which I hoped would make things just a little easier for the lads who had to seek such targets out

Certainly, I had lost so many RAF friends that, when I came to join up, I opted for the Royal Navy, rising to become a petty officer. Then I met a soldier, an officer in the Welch Regiment. We spent just nineteen hours together before the war took him away to Africa and Italy, but immediately he returned, and despite his malaria, dysentery and shellshock, and his father's disappointment that I was not Welsh, we married. He became a canon in Lincoln. And those nineteen hours ushered in fifty-one wonderful years of marriage. Just the same, Geoffrey was the name I chose for my firstborn son.

Over the years I revisited those ghastly sea flats near Boston on several occasions. For a long time the concrete lookout post remained, and a lot of barbed wire. And there, in the stillness, I would simply stand and remember. I would also visit the little cemetery at Coningsby, alongside the aerodrome, where the crew now lie in peace. All but young Terry Davie, their rear gunner, for he rests near his home at Felixstowe. And I would reflect that they had died as they had lived, happy, brave, even carefree, young men when not flying; doing their stern duty steadfastly when they were.

But although memory brings sadness, it also brings renewal. And happiness even. For at Geoff's funeral I met his family, so that later his mother became my son's godmother and Geoff's niece became my goddaughter. In 2004, when his niece visited me with her own husband and son, it was time for a few more tears: sixty-two years on and they too, still remembered; in this case, remembered me ...

As Mrs Davies reveals above, she had always been saddened by the irony that the crew had perished, seemingly pointlessly, as a result of a mechanical – structural – failure. In fact, months before research discovered Mrs Davies, the complementary aspect of the tragedy had emerged.

Throughout all the intervening 65 years, Mrs Edith Houghton, a friend of rear gunner Sergeant James Douglas 'Terry' Davie, had viewed the tragedy from a very different point of view, bound as she had considered herself to be by a promise made between sweethearts. In 2007, however, having had several falls in her home, reading the *Glossop Advertiser* appeal had persuaded her that it was time her story was told.

Mrs Houghton remembered:
As a girl I lived at Stichney, ten miles east of Coningsby. Although christened Edith, I was always called 'Girlie'. At fifteen, despite my youthful appearance, and lying about

Leading Aircraftwoman Edith Borley (later Houghton), 1942.

my age, I applied to enter the Women's Auxiliary Air Force (WAAF). On the first two occasions the recruiting sergeant sent me packing, but on the third he relented – or gave up – so that when I was actually enlisted I had only just turned sixteen. I trained as a telephonist and in the early days had a lot to do with the bomber station at RAF Coningsby.

At times it could be demanding work, so that when operations were on we would switch to twelve-hour shifts. On the other hand, our privileged position meant that we were always party to confidential matters. Also, whenever it interested us, we could winkle out information that should never have come our way!

But non-telephonic information passed too, so that during one of my hurried leaves, Mum and Dad had news for me. 'Girlie,' they told me, 'we've met some very pleasant airmen in the Rose and Crown. They saw your photo and one in particular, Terry Davie, a rear gunner, wants to meet you.'

This sounded promising, but for some time it always fell out that when Terry was free and was able to call at the house, I was away on duty. The time came, though, when we finally met, and the attraction was mutual. From the start he referred to me as his 'little child'. Just the same I became his official/unofficial girlfriend, despite the fact that he had left a childhood sweetheart behind in Felixstowe. As it turned out, I would later meet this girl and find out that Terry had told her that, having met someone else, he would not be returning to her!

I learnt that Terry had done quite a lot of bombing operations. Indeed, he was well into his tour – they had to do thirty ops – and had just two to go. Crews were very close, so as I got to know Terry, I got to know his colleagues reasonably well too.

Many of the Coningsby crews seemed to be an odd mixture. And Terry's was as mixed a bunch as any. There was a Canadian, an Australian and a Scot. Just the same, as a crew they were very much at ease with each other, and towards the end, very proud as well, because their observer, Monty Darvill, and their pilot, a young English flight-sergeant pilot named Geoffrey Appleyard, had both been awarded the Distinguished Flying Medal after raiding Danzig.

One evening we were in the pub with the crowd when Terry made it clear that he had something he wanted to tell me. We found a quiet place outside – on the landlord's seat in the garden – and after swearing me to secrecy, he began to unburden his mind.

'I can't tell anyone else,' he confided, 'but because you're so very special I just want you to know that if we are ever brought down it won't be by the Germans.'

And that is where he would have preferred to leave it. But, of course, I could not let the matter rest there and began to press him. After which, with great reluctance, he went on to explain that the whole crew had become worried about what they saw as their pilot's recently-developed and quite unnecessary recklessness.

As we all knew in that area, having got airborne the bomber force would use the Boston Stump as a marker to set course from. In the last few weeks, it seemed, their pilot had fallen for a girl who lived not far from Boston. Ever since, having got airborne, he would level off not very high up and allow the speed to increase until he came to the girl's house, when he would drop the nose, dive even lower, then pull up sharply, waggling the wings as he did so, only then beginning the climb to the assigned height.

'We've all told him,' Terry said earnestly, 'that pulling back like that, especially while wing wagging, and with all that fuel and all those bombs on board there'll be a day when the bloody kite'll come to bits under the strain. But he won't listen to us.' I remember the way Terry paused then, before conceding, 'Geoff's a brilliant pilot, we appreciate that.' Then, as if ashamed of having to confess it, went on, 'But this new waving-goodbye business of his is getting us all down.'

I could see how deeply this was affecting him. But he had sworn me to secrecy, so rendering me powerless to tell anyone. In my turn, though, I extracted a promise from him.

'Do the crew get any warning that he's going to dive down like that?' I asked. And on being told they did, I urged him, 'Then I want you to promise me that if things go wrong, you'll be ready, and that you'll bale out.'

I pressed even harder, for he too was very special. 'Let the rest go,' I pushed, 'and the aeroplane too, but bale out yourself.'

And in the end, just as I had undertaken to keep my word to him, and to keep his secret even from my parents, so he swore to keep his word to me and to bale out the moment he felt the need to do so.

Perhaps it was a time for sharing secrets, for a day or two later, Archie, the landlord, called me into the garden himself. He was a keen gardener and at the time had an extensive plot of marrows, but he too was clearly uneasy. 'Just look at this,' he directed. And he showed me that, some months before, each member of Terry's crew had scratched his name on one of the marrows. By now, as I could see, the scratches had matured and broadened, so that the names appeared in thick, brownish strokes, as natural growths.

'It was done as a bit of a joke. But increasingly,' he confessed, 'I feel a presentiment. It's as if that crew has fated itself somehow. Only,' he begged, 'don't tell anyone else about these marrows, or about this feeling of mine.' And there was another secret for me to keep.

* * *

Shortly after this I was posted away from the Coningsby area to Biggin Hill, in Kent. But I knew all the communications strings, so whenever Coningsby was on operations I could pull enough of them to reassure myself that Terry was safe. Following the night of 26 July 1942 I once again got myself connected, only to find that no matter how often I called, or how late I checked with the station PBX – the telephone exchange – his crew had not returned.

In fact, even knowing the ropes, it took me another two days of picking up a snatch of gen here and another there, to find out what had happened. But the moment I gathered enough of the story to know that they had not been shot down over Germany but had crashed in Lincolnshire, and just after take-off, I got our sergeant to arrange a forty-eight hour pass for me, pleading the case that I needed to visit my parents.

Dad was an air raid warden with a special responsibility that required him to attend air crashes.

'Where they crashed, Girlie,' he told me, 'was in the Friskney Marshes.' Which meant, I knew, that the aircraft had come down just to the east of both Coningsby and Stickney, and just north-east of Boston.

I'm not sure if Dad realised how close I had become to Terry but when he tried to find out exactly how upset I was I kept a brave face and pretended my interest was just general. Later though, I got one of Dad's colleagues, a man who had actually been among the first on the scene, to describe to me what he had found.

I then discovered that the would-be rescue party had reached the site in the early hours but that, in addition to the normal blackout restrictions, there had been reports that German night-intruders were on the prowl. Consequently, the men could show no lights and had, therefore, been unable to account for the rear gunner: that is, for my Terry. Indeed, it had not been until two days later that they had found Terry's body, some considerable distance from the aircraft.

'The poor devil had baled out before the aircraft actually hit the ground,' Dad's colleague told me, when I pressed for details, 'but he was too low, for every bone in his body was broken.' Then he paused, and said reflectively, 'What a handsome young fellow he was, just the same.'

What a handsome young fellow, indeed! As he still is, in the only photo I ever had of him. And even that was only one I'd had enlarged from a photo taken with some of his crew.

As it was, I applied for two more days off, ultimately angering my sergeant, for while I was unable to admit to him my especial interest, by then he had discovered my practice of contacting Coningsby off my own bat. That side of things, though, hardly weighed with me.

In the course of time I was able to contact Terry's mother, soon after which she came and stayed overnight with us. But I had to be careful, for I could not admit to anyone that

LACW Borley on duty at the Coningsby exchange.

Terry and I had been as close as we had been. Just the same, I think she guessed something and wasn't best pleased. For later, when I stayed overnight with her at Felixstowe, when I went to visit Terry's grave, she wasn't that nice to me.

Perhaps, in part, that was because I turned up accompanied by a soldier. This was because my train had arrived when bombs were actually falling and the soldier, agreeing with me that we were as well off walking rather than staying in the dubious shelter of the train, escorted me to Terry's parents' house. Terry's mother's greeting was something like, 'Oh, you've finally got here, then!' At which the soldier, knowing the strain I had been under, quite apart from the bombs, gave her the rough side of his tongue.

Not the most auspicious start, and she never did warm to me. In particular, I remember she wanted me to wear uniform to the grave and to salute. But that went against the grain. Fortunately, I got on extremely well with Terry's two sisters, Doreen and – I fancy – Noreen, and they lent me their clothes so that I could pay my respects to him in my own way. I was also very affectionately received by Terry's former girlfriend, who was very complimentary, saying that now she could see why Terry had said I was very special.

She, like Terry's mother and everyone who had been associated with the crew, was even more than normally distressed because nobody could tell them why the Lancaster, having safely taken off, had come down so catastrophically just minutes later. But while grieving for them, and along with them, I was bound to secrecy by my promise to my dead sweetheart and was not able to tell anyone, therefore, what I knew. Which was that the pilot had overstressed a heavily-laden, and possibly even a tired, plane. And this is something that I have kept to myself these sixty-plus years.

But life, as it must, went on for us all. More postings followed for me, to Cranwell and to Moreton-in-Marsh, and during the rest of my service I gained a good conduct stripe, eventually leaving the WAAFs as a corporal. Later, I married, although that was a disaster and soon over. Yet I never did tell Terry's secret, then or since.

Only now, as I seem to have become so prone to knocking myself about, it occurs that this might be the last chance to put the record straight for that crew, and indeed for their pilot, Geoff Appleyard. Even for their groundcrew. But especially for Geoff. Remembering that, like Terry, all the crew spoke of his previously careful way of flying. And of the change that had come over him. So the final tragedy must, in itself, have been a reflection of the tremendous strain all of them had been undergoing for so long. Which brings a certain comfort.

31/7/42 Sorties 20; flying hours 119; Pilot. Flight Sergeant Appleyard was the captain of an aircraft detailed to bomb the submarine works at Danzig on the evening of 11/7/42. Owing to the low cloud and poor visibility, he separated from the rest of his formation and proceeded alone from the Danish coast. He did not once see the ground until he came out of the cloud to obtain a pin-point only 30 miles from the target, which was located despite thunderstorms in the gathering darkness. He pressed home his attack below cloud from only 4,000 feet in the face of fierce opposition and he is confident that he scored hits on the primary objective. After bombing, he brought his aircraft down to ground level and shot out 4 searchlights and later took skilful evasive action from 2 fighters. He returned to base after 9.5 hours flying. F/S Appleyard displayed the greatest courage and determination in making this sortie and those same qualities have been much in evidence in the successful completion of numerous other operational sorties.

The London Gazette *of 31 July 1942 recorded that Flight Sergeant Appleyard was awarded the Distinguished Flying Medal for his determination in pressing home an attack on Gdansk, at which time he had logged 119 hours of operational flying and completed 20 operational sorties.*

To date (October 2010) the RAF Museum at Hendon, the repository for surviving air-crash report summaries, has not been able to find a record card for Lancaster R5683. This is not surprising, however, for many went missing during those years of audits when nobody supposed they would be of further interest. On the other hand it is conceivable that The National Archives at Kew may still have the full report. However, the authoritative *Bomber Command Losses* series has R5683 'exploding in the air'.

Good enough, of course, as a one-line summary of the cause. But the first arrivals at the crash site spoke of a compact and intense conflagration. Which suggests that the aircraft, in fact, suffered a catastrophic failure in the air at low level but actually exploded on impact: a scenario fully consistent with a tired airframe at near all-up-weight having suffered a too-sharp rolling-'g' snatch applied with an overabundance of *joie de vivre*. And fully consistent with an experienced rear gunner's only too starkly realised fear. A fear which had to be expressed. If only in secret.

And what a secret to have protected all those years!

The inauguration of the Appleyard Room, RAF Coningsby, 31 October 2007. Mrs Kathleen Davies, seated, with Mrs Judith Brewer, niece of Flight Sergeant Appleyard, DFM. Hosts, No. 106 Squadron.

10

Pathfinder Nights

Warrant Officer Harry Parker, DFM
flight engineer

In the last few years I suppose I have become a relatively familiar figure at Derbyshire's Ladybower Dam Museum, talking about Pathfinder Nights to the visiting schoolchildren. The surroundings and knowing what part the Derwent Dams played in the war waged by their grandfathers whets their imagination. Certainly the interest is there, despite the passage of time, and sad though some may find such an interest …

For me, the involvement in that now-distant war started in 1941 when a change of rules allowed me to seek a release from the steel industry in order to fly with the RAF. The tribunal approved my application so that as I approached eighteen I found myself at the aircrew selection centre at RAF Cardington, near Bedford, undergoing medicals and aptitude tests. In the days beforehand I had vacillated between asking to become a pilot and following my bent for engineering. But there was no real decision to be made, for although I was found 'suitable PNB' (pilot, navigator and bomb aimer) my background made me perfect material for the newly-established aircrew category of flight engineer. First though, came eight weeks of general service training in Blackpool.

In fact, as far as doing my bit was concerned, I might as well have opted for pilot training, for it transpired that I was to play the guinea pig, and mine would take very nearly as long. Having done a full ground mechanic's course at St Athan, in Wales, my intake were then required to complete the more demanding ground-fitter's course at Halton, in Buckinghamshire, only then returning to St Athan to embark upon our flight engineer's course proper. A wasteful procedure, but one which set the pattern for the tailored-to-suit aircrew engineer's courses of the future. And as it happened, the seemingly unnecessary in-depth training was to stand me in good stead in post-war job hunting!

I finished this phase of training with a brevet and sergeant's stripes but I was also put forward for a commission. The board, however, managed to put my socialist back up, accordingly I thanked them, and returned to the sergeant's mess where there were no mess bills to set against the pound a day I was receiving.

Twenty shiny shillings a day, and all found! Just the same, this was defrayed, for the government had lowered the personal allowance on income tax to help pay for the war; post-war credits, they called it. Although many years after the war – as late as 1973! – we got back what we'd paid in (always provided, that is, we'd kept hold of our post-war-credit certificates!) the beggars totally discounted the accrued interest!

Regarding commissioning, Alex Thorne, my pilot, was to nag me incessantly. 'The CO'll sign it up right away, you know that,' he'd urge. But I stuck to my guns and I never regretted it. After all, rank meant nothing in the air, and little enough on the ground; off duty, at any rate.

My first aircrew posting was to No. 1663 Conversion Unit at RAF Rufforth, near York, then operating Halifaxes. Shortly after arriving I was approached by Alex, the flight lieutenant pilot just mentioned, who, after a brief chat, asked me to join his crew. Until that time he and the lads had been training on Wellingtons but now, converting to heavies, they needed a flight engineer. I acquiesced, and it could not have been a more serendipitous coming together, for from the start we all got on well, not particularly living in each other's pockets on the ground but forming a superb relationship in the air.

We were a heterogeneous bunch. Alex, the pilot – and therefore, captain – was debonair and tailor-made for the public relations world he came from. Additionally, and far from the norm in crew constituency, there were four other officers: Graham Rose, very self-contained and a brilliant and conscientious navigator; Boris Bresslof, our navigator (radar), a Jewish hairdresser from London; and Reg Keary, our bomb aimer, a bank teller. The final officer was the rear gunner, Jim Raymont, a Birmingham jeweller. The senior NCOs comprised me; James (another Jim) Crabtree, our wireless operator/air gunner, a police cadet from Rochdale; and Jock Scott, our mid-upper gunner. Well! What to say about Jock! He was a Gallowgate Glaswegian, had a very short fuse, and was forever getting tight. But – arguably his only saving grace – he was a very good air gunner.

The Rufforth course was a busy one for all crew members, but especially so for the pilot and flight engineer. Not only that, but it saw me getting my feet off the ground for the first time!

We started off with innumerable circuits of the airfield. These were mainly to get the pilot's eye in, but on take-off, when Alex relinquished the throttles in order to have both hands on the wheel, I would ensure that they did not vibrate back. Then, on landing, I would do various bits and pieces he called for, putting down the flaps and, just before the wheels touched, easing off the power. Indeed, judging the latter often made or marred the touchdown!

The airborne exercises invariably involved stopping one or more of the four engines, sometimes when carrying out steep turns. Even in level flight stopping an engine caused a sizeable swinging effect which the pilot might well have his work cut out to contain. The flight engineer then, would invariably be called upon to switch off the fuel and ignition and turn the now windmilling propeller blades to give minimum opposition to the airflow; to feather them, that is. All this, while keeping an eye on the gauges crowding his panel and reflecting the well-being, or otherwise, of the aircraft systems as a whole. There were times, in fact, when several more arms – to say nothing of eyes and ears – might have been useful. More especially when the instructor introduced us to flying on just two engines. As if we would ever need to fly with just two engines on an aircraft which the far-seeing manufacturer had provided with four!

We also did several practice-bombing and air-to-air and air-to-ground gunnery sorties, as well as navigational exercises, my log book showing a total of sixty-two hours' flying time by the end of the course.

Once signed off from Rufforth, we moved to No. 8 Group's Navigation Training Unit at RAF Warboys near Chatteris, in Huntingdonshire, where we converted onto the Lancaster, concentrating on flying mock operations and bomb dropping.

As the Lancaster had only one pilot, flight engineers were given a dozen or so hours in the Link trainer ground-simulator learning to fly straight and level. Of course, there was no thought of our attempting a landing, but it did mean that, should the pilot be incapacitated, someone aboard could fly the rest of the crew back to Britain where they could bale out without becoming prisoners of war or risk drowning uselessly in the Channel. For many flight engineers the Link sessions were the end of it but on our crew, when we were returning from ops and things were quiet, Alex would often shift from his seat and let me fly the aircraft for a while.

Certainly our cohesion under his leadership must have been noted, for even before training ended we were asked if we would join Pathfinder Force. Naturally we grabbed at the chance, reporting to RAF Downham Market, in Norfolk, to join No. 635 Pathfinder Squadron with whom we were to do a near-tour-and-a-half, and in my case, fifty-five ops.

Having joined the squadron – Motto: 'We lead, others follow' – our personal flying logbooks began to fill with names that still do something to the blood; so many of them logged in red to record night raids against Germany's industrial Ruhr. Our first operation, however, in August 1944, was against a V1 Flying Bomb site in France, a day raid and logged, therefore, in green. The next op took us to a railway junction at Lens, in Belgium, and the third to the Opel works in Russelheim where, in the course of our pathfinding, we descended from 19,000 to 16,000 feet, additionally dropped four 2,000 pound bombs, then spent ten minutes trying to escape not only from searchlights but also from two enemy fighters Jim Raymont had spotted.

Some of our early ops were in support of the army, then trying to break clear of the Invasion beachhead, a memorable briefing for one of them being given by our commanding officer, Wing Commander Stanley 'Tubby' Baker.

'Chaps,' he announced, 'the troops are bogged down at Falaise. The other air force' – he meant the Yanks – 'has made a cock-up. If you do the same, don't bother coming back.'

Even though we began our tour in the summer, the weather was always a factor, especially when it forced a recall after the force had got airborne. For a start, such trips did not count as ops. More importantly they represented a lot of wasted energy; not least, I suspect, of the hidden, nervous variety.

Wing Commander Stanley 'Tubby' Baker, DSO and bar, DFC and bar.

Just one of the regrettable things about aborted ops was that the bombs had to be jettisoned in designated areas in the sea. It might seem unnecessarily profligate, particularly considering the dangers run by the munitions workers in constructing the things. But cookies, as an example, were nothing but dustbins full of dynamite; no fins, no finesse. At the best of times all very well if they dropped clear when released over the target, but you didn't want them being banged around in the bomb bay when a tired pilot was trying to bring off a landing.

On one occasion after a recall Alex was settled into the approach for Downham Market's runway when 'Tubby' Baker called from control, 'Thorne, have you jettisoned your bombs?'

'No, sir,' Alex replied calmly, maintaining his descent, 'I thought we'd save 'em for next time.'

'Then bugger off out to sea and get rid of them,' the CO snapped. 'I'm not having you blowing up my airfield.'

And so we overshot, and headed back for the sea, for although Alex was a press-on type he was not one of those fatal 'press on *regardless*' ones. Most definitely not.

* * *

Target indicators coming down.

In September 1944, we marked for a main-force raid on Boulogne-sur-Mer, in the Pas de Calais, doing two daylight runs across the target. A few days later we were over gun positions at Calais itself, placing eight target indicators but additionally dropping six 1,000 pound bombs.

The target indicators mentioned – 'Tee Eyes', in the parlance – were dropped by pathfinder aircraft some minutes before the main bomber force began to arrive. The master bomber would then assess their accuracy and direct the main force accordingly, intoning 'Bomb on the green Tee Eyes'. If the target indicators proved to be inaccurately laid, or if they drifted off target, he would drop replacement indicators, updating his instructions and ordering, 'Do not bomb on the green Tee Eyes, bomb on the red Tee Eyes – bomb on the *red* markers.' All very taut, despite the studiously laconic tone one grew to expect.

And taut, because for all one heard tell of 'milk-runs' it was held as axiomatic on our crew that there was no such thing. However, what has to count as one of our hairiest sorties was the op we flew on 6 October 1944.

We were raiding Gelsenkirchen in the Ruhr when two of our engines were shot out by flak. And yes, how we thanked our 'as-if-this-could-ever-happen' Rufforth training then! Having feathered the affected props we made our way back towards the sea, except that, as we coasted out, so flak caught us yet again, this time damaging one of the control rods to the starboard rudder. Initially the rudder flopped about loosely, but then it jammed, causing a yawing force, so that I had to take the fire-axe to the rear and sever the damaged rod.

We finally made it to the North Sea but although Alex ordered us to prepare for ditching, we knew he would try everything else before putting down on the sea. The truth being that Alex hated water! To such an extent that he had always tried to short-cut the periodic dinghy drills. Once the rest of us had righted the upturned dinghy, Alex, dryshod and poised on the edge of the pool, would leap aboard. Except that the instructor got wise and just as Water-Hater jumped, yanked on the rope, pulling the dinghy away and leaving Alex to fume and splutter back to the side.

Now though, we descended inexorably over the sea as Graham brought us to a landfall near Woodbridge, the very long and very wide emergency airfield in Suffolk. Only just as we committed ourselves to the approach, so the port-outer engine failed. And now, on just one engine, already that low, with wheels and flaps down, we could do nothing but sink into a field some way short of the runway, taking out some power cables for good measure but coming to a halt before demolishing a cottage.

There were two distinct impacts after touchdown. And by the second one flames were everywhere. Earlier, when Alex had called us to our crash stations, Jim Raymont had come forward from his rear turret. Now, in a brief moment of farce, he complained that he couldn't see. 'Then take your sunglasses off,' I told him shortly.

In fact, Jim may have been better off back in his turret – it is always problematical in such cases – for on the first impact the aircraft had broken its back, the whole rear section carrying away, turret and all, without catching fire.

Alex, I could see, was pretty groggy. On the Lancaster there was a bar above the pilot's head to enable him to haul himself up when leaving the seat. Alex had been jarred roofwards by the impact and cracked his head on the bar. Dazed as he was, however, he had finally managed to extricate himself from his seat and go rearwards with nav-radar Boris, only to find the flames too fierce. Turning back, the two of them evacuated from the front instead.

For my part I had banged my shoulder quite badly. Nevertheless, despite the flames, I got through the already-jettisoned top hatch, only to have some fuel suddenly flare up and blow me off the wing. I picked myself up and began to run towards the cottage, knowing we needed help. As I reached the fence, I saw a bicycle propped up against the wall and I could think of nothing but pedalling off to alert Woodbridge. Only then, looking up, I saw that the crash crews were already speeding our way.

My head having cleared a bit, I gave up the bike idea and ran back to the aircraft, now a blazing wreck. One of the crash squad approached and asked me if I knew where the missing crew member was. And for the first time I realised that Jim Crabtree, our WOp/AG, was not in the survivor's group huddled beyond the wreck. Hurriedly thinking back I could only deduce that he had jettisoned the top hatch and exited at some time before I had. With that in mind I began to lead the crash crew to where I thought he might be. But then I caught sight of a mound under the white-hot wreckage. And I could go no further. And that was that.

Except that amidst all the turmoil the old lady from the cottage appeared with a napkin-covered tray, offering us all drinks from a bone-china tea service.

The court of inquiry concluded that, thinking the first impact meant that the aircraft had stopped, Jim had left his crash station and got half way through the hatch, only to have the second impact throw him clear, after which part of the structure had come down and crushed him. Hopefully, I like to think, before the flames took hold.

We were given leave, but the ops programming was relentless, and a fortnight later we were back on the battle order, joined now by Sergeant Ernest 'Ernie' Patterson, a former jobbing builder from Darlington, our new wireless operator/air gunner.

So it was off to Essen, and back to eyeing a sky that was rapidly filling with flak. 'It's impossible to get through that lot,' I'd think, but then, as the distance lessened, gaps would appear. Alex worked on the theory that if one lot of flak had burst without effect the gunners would change their settings, so he would steer for the brightest cluster. Hardly defensible logic, but it served us well.

Then, on 28 October 1944, we raided Cologne, dropping ten target indicators. I can't recall anything out of the ordinary about that trip but on landing Alex received an

Post-raid photo of Cologne, October 1944.

immediate Distinguished Flying Cross. Probably, though, this was in recognition of a series of ops, and not least for his tenacity during the sortie culminating in the tragedy at Woodbridge.

As the months went on, so we progressed through the Pathfinder ranks, if hastened not a little by losses. For losses, of course, were inevitable. Very often we would lose one or two Lancasters, on occasion we might lose many more. Ten, seventeen, eleven, thirteen... When acting as master bomber over Dessau on 18 March 1945 we lost eighteen, and having raided Chemnitz, on 7 March 1945, twenty-two Lancasters failed to return. Twenty-two, each with at least seven men on board!

As a first step in our advancement we began to act as the primary visual marker, laying down the target indicators for major raids on Düsseldorf, Bochum and Gelsenkirchen. Then we did our first trip as deputy master bomber, to Walcheren, in Holland's Scheldt Estuary, where the aim was to breach the dykes. This short initiation in raid-controlling took us just over two hours.

Finally, in March 1945, we took centre stage as master bomber, in short order raiding Dorsten, Osnabrück, Nüremburg, Munich, Kiel, and the oil refinery at Hamburg, most of the sorties taking between five and eight hours. And on the Nüremburg raid in particular, on 11 April 1945, we were well and truly shot up while orbiting the target area.

In all conscience, there was little sweetness and light around during ops, but limping home, obviously in trouble and being gradually outdistanced by everyone else and so made even more vulnerable, it gave us pleasure to find that an American Mustang long-range escort fighter had elected to sit at our wingtip! More, because its black pilot had thrown back his canopy and was puffing away at a cigar that dwarfed any of Churchill's. Clearly too, he had radioed ahead, for as we cleared the Channel and he dived off with a cheery wave, so three Spitfires slipped into position to escort us the rest of way to Downham.

One tends to forget, and the logbooks record little more than the facts. Yet so many things happened. The time, for instance, when Alex turned off the runway too enthusiastically and so thoroughly bogged us down that we needed a tractor to tow us out. Or when we received frantic after-landing signals to stop dead, the groundcrew having realised that our million candle-power post-drop photo-flare had hung up on us over the target and had been dangling beneath the fuselage ever since. It transpired that its releasing pin had been bent and hadn't pulled free, making us even more of a potential fireball than normal.

But there had been an equally notable hang-up moment. As normal, just before stopping engines, we had opened the bomb doors: if this wasn't done the groundcrew lads would have to wind them open manually. Anyway, Jock Scott – he of the short fuse – was first out of the aircraft, to be discovered, as the rest of us emerged, angrily rounding on one of the armourers.

'Prithee, Sire,' was clearly the burden of his discontent, 'why have you brought this 500 pound bomb and rolled it into position ready for loading when we are still on board?'

But that was Jock. To everyone else it was chillingly apparent that the thing had failed to drop clear over the target but had come adrift later and had been banging about in the bomb bay all the way back. Until we had opened the bomb-bay doors, that is, and it had deposited itself, egg-like, onto the tarmac.

Fortunately, it been one of those loaded towards the rear of the bomb bay. For the air-driven spinner vane needed only one revolution to withdraw the striker and make the bomb live, and with the tailwheeled Lanc sitting rose high on the tarmac, the greater fall from the front of the bomb bay would have been quite sufficient to do that, when the whole bloody lot of us would have gone up. But then bombs were always touchy things. Even touchier than our Jock.

Another hang up though, actually proved productive. On that occasion we had been tasked to mark for a raid on the submarine base at Stettin, in Norway. It was a lengthy flog, so having been routed across neutral Sweden to save distance, we were not overly surprised when their anti-aircraft gunners opened up on us. What did surprise us was their poor aim; absolutely spot on for height, but way off laterally. Alex sent down a light-

Bombs being prepared, showing the spinner vanes (white) inside the fins.

hearted call telling them this, receiving the complacent response that they were well aware of it!

Having done the job at Stettin, one of our 500 pound bombs hung up. On the way back, however, we cured the fault and when, by pure chance, we overflew a battleship, we let the bomb go and actually scored a hit.

It turned out that our opportunity target had been the SMS *Schleswig-Holstein*. Though a participant at Jutland in the First World War, she had been so antiquated that, under the Armistice conditions, Germany had been permitted to keep her. Then, on 1 September 1939, having been positioned at Westerplatte, Gdansk, for an ostensible friendship visit, she had opened fire on the Polish garrison, so ushering in the Second World War. Our bomb merely damaged her, but some weeks later British aircraft sent her to the bottom.

An op that readily comes to mind was our raid on Osnabrück as master bomber. We boarded and prepared to start engines, only to find that no fuel had been loaded. There was a hiatus, but then we changed aeroplanes. Except that on this one the voice radio was dead: no good for a master bomber! Then a fuel bowser appeared... By now the pathfinders had long gone. Just the same, after Alex and Graham had put their heads together, and though forty-five minutes late, we ignored the briefed strategic routing and set off on an unheard of straight line track for Osnabrück, running into a spot of bother crossing the Dortmund-Ems canal, but arriving moments before the pathfinders and exactly on time to assess their marking. All very gratifying!

Some weeks later, Alex was at home on leave when he was notified of his DSO: his Distinguished Service Order. Checking back, he found that it had been awarded for an otherwise unexceptionable operation. A congratulatory note enclosed with the notification explained this: 'We couldn't cite the Osnabrück saga, we can't endorse mistakes!'

I loosely spoke of an 'unexceptionable operation'. In fact, none fell into that category. We did, however, make a bit of a joke about Alex's keenness. As we finished our jobs, and as the rest of us were mentally turning onto a course for home, he would invariably chirp up with, 'As master bomber we ought to get the best possible photo,' and off he'd take us into yet another flak-filled orbit. Whatever had gone on before, this invariably seemed to spur on the hatefulness from below. At which, as the shells burst all around us, I'd say, 'You've bloody done it again, Alex, haven't you!'

As I have said, our crew did not believe in milk-runs. Just the same there was a move to reckon operational duty in terms of points rather than tours, five points for a German target, only three for a French one, so clearly the powers that be themselves subscribed to the 'easy-target' concept! This though, went above our heads, for having reached our thirty ops – the normal first tour for Bomber Command main force at that time – we simply carried on, flying our last-ever operation on 18 April 1945. Nor had things got less fraught by then, for just two trips before that, flak over the target had taken out one of our engines. And on 8 May 1945 the war in Europe was over.

When detailed for their last flight, the rest of the lads had done 53 ops, but some months earlier I had flown with another crew and got one up on them. Unwilling, therefore, to let them fly with a strange flight engineer on their final sortie, I went along, so notching up a personal tally of 55 operational sorties. In doing so I had flown a total of 221 hours by day and 160 by night.

On being posted from the squadron I was sent to an aircrew disposal unit at Catterick, basically to be remustered into some other Service occupation. However, in June 1945, having asked to continue flying, I was posted to Ringwood in the New Forest, Hampshire, to engage in trials during which gliders would be snatched from the ground by that twin-engined workhorse, the Dakota.

A Dakota approaching the suspended cable to snatch the Hadrian (the Waco, to the Americans) glider.

It was the Far East, of course, where many of the forces released in Europe were to be sent. Only extracting casualties from the vast areas of thick jungle was recognised as a major problem, hence the decision to use gliders.

The method required a large loop, fashioned in the unattached end of the glider's tow cable, to be suspended twelve feet from the ground. The Dakota tug, fitted with a hydraulically operated hook, would be held to near ground level, overfly the glider, then engage the suspended loop. With both engines already roaring at full power the Dakota would take up the slack then drag the glider steeply into the air, the climb angle being gamely assisted by the glider pilots. Pilots plural, because the glider's envisaged behind-the-lines role made a single pilot so vulnerable to small-arms fire.

It was far too risky to use real troops for the trials, so the Hadrian gliders – Wacos to the Americans – were ballasted with lumps of concrete. At some three and half tons, however, they were was almost half the weight of a Dakota, so that any straight snatch would have ripped the poor old tug in half. For this reason a device was fitted to ease the snatch-shock.

My part came after the glider had released itself from the tug and the Dakota pilot had retracted the hook. I would stretch out before the open cargo door, reach back into the slipstream with a boathook, unsnag the cable from the hook and draw it inboard so that it could be safely deposited on the strip.

If I was lucky, I would have someone to hold onto my ankles as I stretched out into infinity. Even then, I felt distinctly exposed. Especially as our whimsical pilots loved choosing the decisive moment to bank hard over, so presenting the open door – and the new chum, me! – to the ground.

Discounting that, few of these trials-cum-training sorties proved devoid of interest in their own right. The venue was Ibsley, a short hop from Ringwood, and surrounded by woodlands. When we lost an engine shortly after take-off therefore, the New Forest was all set to swallow up both tug and glider. There was, however, a rather suspect, and decidedly unpredictable, cable-severing device. 'Shall I fire the cable cutter?' I yelled. 'No,' the pilot yelled back, 'it might blow the bloody tail off.' At which the engine roared back into life again and we were able to resume breathing.

As it happened, the atom bombs were dropped and the Japanese gave up, therefore I wasn't called upon to actually try out this derring-do technique over mountainous, jungle-covered terrain. Instead I could finally contemplate a quiet life.

Group Captain Leonard Cheshire discussing Mosquito technicalities.

First, though, I had to find a job. A problem temporarily solved when Alex, now secretary of the Pathfinder Club, rang to say that he had recommended me to Group Captain Leonard Cheshire who was seeking a flight engineer with ground qualifications: my so-protracted training at Halton and St Athan finally bearing fruit! When we met, Cheshire told me that he was planning a tour of the Continent, fund-raising for the care homes he wanted to set up. As transport he had brought two de Havilland Mosquitoes – two for £750! Would I help him with them? Having heard so much about him, and being so impressed at this first meeting, I accepted on the spot.

My first task was to travel to Montrose, in Scotland, and get the two semi-mothballed aircraft ready for flight. On arrival I found that Cheshire had arranged pretty near carte blanche on labour for any special skills the task required his forethought meaning that the job was done in record time. The two of us then did a double ferry to get the Mosquitoes down to Marshalls of Cambridge where they were certificated and entered upon the civilian register.

Over the next few months, with me still wearing uniform, although by then I was officially out of the RAF, we flew to virtually every major European city and to many American bases. Throughout, Cheshire proved to be an absolute gentleman. Certainly, I can say of Leonard Cheshire, as I can say about no other man, that he had absolutely no side, that he was equally at ease with fellow pilot Prince Bernhard of the Netherlands – encountered on the tarmac at Basle – as with a hotel porter. Indeed, his quality shines through in the letter of recommendation he furnished me with when the tour ended. Regrettably creased for all its plastic sleeve, it is a document I continue to treasure.

When discussing our time as operational aircrew, people often ask how we coped with fear. And indeed, fear was probably ever-present at some level. But in our crew I believe we coped by concentrating on the job in hand. Certainly, I remember Graham, our navigator, plotting away on a night when flak was filling the night sky as never before. 'Just look at that lot,' I gritted. 'Can't at the moment, Harry,' he told me, his pencil never wavering, 'this calculation's just a little tricky.' For there was always something to do, to check and double-check, be it a gauge, a calculation or the hostile skies beyond.

One of the truly fearful things, of course, was to see other aircraft going down. On 25 October 1944, for instance, we saw two Lancasters, each hit by flak, both spiralling earthwards at the same time. Then again, in November 1944, a Lancaster blew up virtually underneath us, toppling us over so far that I had to help Alex right us. Shortly after that, over Heligoland, two Lancasters collided just in front of us. What was utterly hideous, though, was when the downed aircraft fell in flames.

Flak was, of course, a natural concomitant to all bombing operations, and to Pathfinder operations in particular. Even more so when acting as deputy or master bomber, tasks which called for spending thirty minutes or more dwelling over the target.

The barrel of the V3 rocket-boosted long-range cannon.

As the directing bomber circled so the German radars below would have this one blip chasing its tail as the rest of the stream was scurrying on its way. The blip would also be the only one transmitting! Naturally, it was the blip that came in for the most particular attention.

The case, indeed, on 25 March 1945 when we were the blip. As we began our third orbit four bracketing shells exploded immediately below us, causing so much damage that on landing we needed a new wing tank and bomb bay door. Even then, on the way back, Alex had to force the controls through some restriction or other after they began to jam.

Then again, sooner or later, the master, radar-controlled searchlight would seek us out. It wasn't white like the others, but off-white: get caught in that and the rest would be onto you in seconds! What saved us was realising that it didn't seem able to sweep the whole arc of the sky. Instead, it would come up to ninety degrees and then have to swing back and start again, at which point we would dive like fury away from it, corkscrewing as we went.

Another thing people often ask about is the post-war vilification of our bombing campaign. There were wartime objectors too, although not many to be found in the streets, where people thanked us for demolishing so many V1 flying-bomb sites and urged us to do the same for the V2 rockets. Powerless to contain the latter, which had no fixed launching sites, we did, at least, prevent the V3 rocket-boosted long-range cannon from coming into action!

And although post-war studies revealed much about the inaccuracy of aerial bombing – in a sense, good old hindsight! – the wild inaccuracy of both German V-weapons were known to their High Command even as they were launched. And launched by the thousand! It should not be forgotten, either, that after the invasion the Allied bombing strategy changed markedly. Even then, there are so many issues…

What I can say, however, as crew, is that on ops, even at the darkest moments, as flak burst all around us and we craned downwards, doing our level best to ensure that the markers were indeed over the specific target we had been sent to bomb; while aware that there must of necessity be – as it is now euphemistically termed – collateral damage; at such times I would reflect that out of all the horror something better must emerge. And if I was, perhaps, a little naïve, I was also very young, but I really did trust that when the war was over we would emerge into a significantly better world.

* * *

The crew, taken before the crash at Woodbridge, but listed with decorations at the war's end. Left to right: *Squadron Leader Alex Thorne, DSO, DFC, pilot; Flight Lieutenant Graham Rose, DFC, navigator; Flight Lieutenant Boris Bresslof, DFC, navigator (radar); Pilot Officer James (Jimmy) Crabtree, wireless operator/air gunner (killed at Woodbridge); Warrant Officer Jock Scott, DFM, mid-upper gunner; Pilot Officer Jim Raymont, DFC, rear gunner; Warrant Officer Harry Parker, DFM, flight engineer. (Pilot Officer Reg Keary, DFC, bomb aimer, is absent).*

Back in 1945, standing down from ops, coupled with VE Day, meant the parting of the ways for the crew. Not that we had ever been of the 'closer than kin' variety. Off duty we had tended to go our separate ways, but on duty we really had made a formidable team.

We had also been well treated. Although we were not entitled to the Aircrew Europe Star, having started ops after D-Day, each of us had been awarded a decoration that evidenced his service in the air, Alex, as our leader, doubly so, receiving not only a DFC but also a DSO.

And so we left the RAF. Alex, now a squadron leader, returned to what became known as PR, his public-relations junketings taking him far and wide. He also had his serious side. For ten years he was editor of *Air Mail*, the magazine of the RAF Association charity, and as mentioned he was secretary of the Pathfinder Club. He also wrote a very good book [Thorne, Alex, (1990) *Lancaster at War 4: Pathfinder Squadron*, Middlesex: Ian Allan].

Graham Rose returned to Reading University to complete the degree he had given up to become a navigator and ended up staying on as a don. Boris Bresslof, being Jewish, was particularly gratified to have escaped the sort of confrontation being shot down might have led to. Once out of uniform he rejoined his brother in their hairdressing establishment in London.

Harry Parker in 2009

Reg Keary, always something of an unknown quantity, returned to his bank. Ernie Patterson married former landgirl Kay, whom he had met in our off-duty stamping ground of Wisbech, and went back to being a jobbing builder in Darlington. Jimmy Raymont, already married with two children when he signed on as aircrew, quietly returned to his jewellery business in Birmingham.

Jock Scott, alone, we never heard from afterwards. I can only presume that he returned to Glasgow and continued blowing his top and drinking himself into oblivion.

As for me, having left Leonard Cheshire I got a job with a firm constructing diggers and dumpers, my associated comings and goings being overseen from the office by Eileen, who, long before I had moved on to manage a firm in St Albans, was able to organise me during fifty-four years of the very happiest of marriages.

So many happy years! And when it had to end the epitaph I inscribed for Eileen was the tenet we had long lived by, 'We may never see tomorrow, there's no written guarantee...'

It summed up our philosophy in marriage. Yet, thinking back, how much it applied too, to the life I had lived in those wartime years.

Certainly they had introduced me to a world beyond the narrow confines of my upbringing. Meeting and mixing with Cheshire was a case in point, but only one of many. I do not think I was ever all that diffident a youth, but after my Service experiences I found I had not the least fear of life, or of the challenges it offers. Not least its partings.

And there have been partings, even though our crew has continued to meet over the years, with just Jock falling by the way, and with only the diminution of death weeding out the rest of us. But as I write in 2010 three of us remain, me, Ernie and Boris, and we continue to visit. Indeed, we have even become celebrities, and are sought out by the Aces High organisation, which collects us from our homes, feeds us royally, and sets us to signing books and memorabilia!

All good fun, and so gratifying to rediscover at each venue that, like the children at the Derwent Dam Museum, so many people of generations that were yet to be born when we were airborne over Germany are still interested in the air war that was fought out on their behalf during those now so far off days.

Aircraft Types

The details given below are subject to the caveat that any performance figures can only be a rough guide. Indeed, flying any one of a line-up of a given aircraft type will show all such data to be merely representative.

Allied machines

Airspeed Oxford

The 1937 twin-engined, wooden-framed, plywood-skinned Airspeed Oxford remained in RAF Service until 1954. This dual-controlled general purpose trainer had a basic crew of three but could accommodate other trainee-aircrew depending upon the role.

Two 375 horsepower Armstrong Siddeley Cheetah Ten radial engines, or alternatively, two 450 horsepower Pratt & Whitney radial engines, gave it a maximum speed of 188 mph (163 knots), a cruising speed of 163 mph (142 knots), and a ceiling of 19,000 feet; range was 700 miles.

It could carry practice bombs, and an early version had a dorsal turret with a single 0.303 inch (7.7 mm) calibre machine gun.

Armstrong Whitworth Whitley

The 1936 five-crewed, twin-engined Whitley bomber was withdrawn from Bomber Command operations in April 1942 but served on in the training, maritime, paratrooping, clandestine-operations and glider-tug roles.

Most variants were powered by two 1,145 horsepower Rolls-Royce Merlin in-line engines. Performance is not that easy to establish as contemporary figures were subject to propaganda, estimates of the cruising speed varying from 210 mph (183 knots) down to 165 mph (143 knots) and as low as 120 mph (104 knots). Even the service ceiling of 26,000 feet seems suspect.

Typical armament was a single 0.303 inch (7.7 mm) calibre machine gun in the nose, and four in a tail turret. The bomb load was 7,000 pounds over a range of 1,500 miles. The photo demonstrates the Whitley's characteristic low-nose 'sit'; it is flying level but at high speed.

Avro Anson

The 1935 Avro Anson maritime reconnaissance aircraft remained in RAF service until 1968, a twenty-two year span, many being built in Canada. Withdrawn from operational service in early 1942, it was then extensively employed as a trainer for all aircrew specialisations. The normal crew varied from three to five, but it could be configured as an eight- to eleven-seat classroom or communications aircraft. The Anson was well liked by those who flew it, being easy to fly, dependable, sturdy and relatively forgiving.

Typically powered by two 350 horsepower Armstrong Siddeley Cheetah Nine radial engines, it had a cruising speed of 158 mph (138 knots), a ceiling of 19,000 feet, and a range of nearly 800 miles.

Its design-role armament was two 0.303 inch calibre (7.7 mm) machine-guns; a fixed, forward-firing Vickers, and a single Lewis in a dorsal turret. The nose had a bomb-aimer's station and 360 pounds of bombs could be carried.

Avro Lancaster

The seven-crewed Lancaster, developed from the twin-engined Manchester, first flew in January 1941. Designed for ease of production and subsequent servicing, 7,737 were built by 1946.

Powered by four 1,640 horsepower Rolls-Royce Merlin Mk.24 in-line engines, its maximum speed was 280

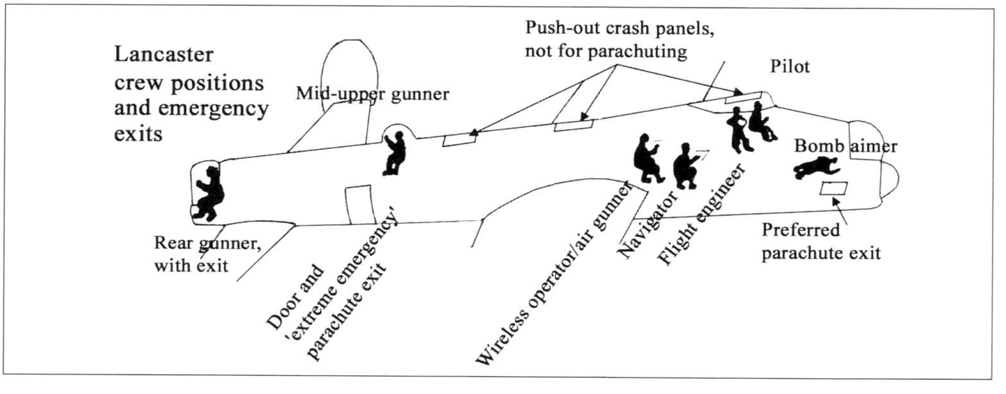

mph (243 knots), it cruised at 210 mph (182 knots) or, on three engines, at 140 mph (122 knots), operating up to 22,000 feet over a range of 2,500 miles. The standard bomb load was 14,000 pounds – for a comparison often made, the Flying Fortress's standard load was 6,000 pounds – or, if modified, one of 22,000 pounds. Armament was eight, 0.303 inch (7.7 mm) calibre machine guns; four in the tail, and two each in nose and dorsal turrets.

B-24 Consolidated Liberator

Over 18,000 B-24 Liberator long-range heavy bomber and maritime reconnaissance machines were built during the Second World War, the production rate reaching one every fifty-six minutes. Variously crewed depending upon the role, they were commonly manned by eight to ten crew.

Typically powered by four 1,200 horsepower Pratt and Whitney Twin Wasp engines driving Curtiss three-bladed, electrically driven, constant-speed propellers, the Liberator had a maximum speed of 280 mph (243 knots), a cruising speed of 220 mph (191 knots), and a ceiling of 36,000 feet. It had a range of 2,500 miles, and could carry 8,000 pounds of bombs, or 12,800 pounds up to 990 miles.

Armament varied with the mark, but was typically nine 0.5 inch (12.7 mm) calibre machine guns, two in nose, dorsal and tail turrets, one in each waist position, and one in the ventral – belly – position..

Boeing Stearman, Model 75

The Stearman (Boeing) 75 Series Kaydet biplane trainer was widely used in the USA and Canadian flying schools during the Second World War.

Its 220 horsepower Continental R-670-5 engine gave it a maximum speed of 124 mph (108 knots), and a ceiling of 11,200 feet. It had a range of 505 miles.

Boulton Paul Defiant

The dorsal – on the back – turret of the 1937 low-wing, all-metal, twin-crewed Boulton Paul Defiant was meant to give it an advantage over fighters limited to fixed, forward-firing guns. In fact, the turret caused so much drag that that the machine never reached an acceptable standard and in August 1940 it was withdrawn from daylight operations. Once equipped with airborne-interception radar and re-employed as a night-fighter it was more successful. Later it was used as a target tug.

A 1,280 horsepower Rolls-Royce Merlin Mk.20 in-line engine gave a cruising speed of 260 mph (226 knots) and a ceiling of 30,000 feet. The range was 465 miles.

The turret carried four 0.303 inch (7.7 mm) calibre machine guns with no fixed guns.

Bristol Beaufighter

The two-seater Beaufighter was initially employed as an airborne interception-equipped night-fighter. It also served Coastal Command as a long-range strike fighter and torpedo carrier.

Typically, two 1,770 horsepower Bristol Hercules radial engines gave a maximum speed of 303 mph (263 knots), a cruising speed of 249 mph (216 knots), and a ceiling of 15,000 feet. Range was 1,470 miles.

A common armament fit was four forward-firing, nose-mounted 20 mm (0.79 inch) calibre Hispano cannon and six forward-firing, wing-mounted Browning 0.303 inch (7.7 mm) calibre machine guns with a single Vickers in the rear. Each cannon gave a rate of fire of 550 shells a minute, and each machine gun 1,100 rounds a minute.

Either a 2,127 pound torpedo could be carried or one of 1,605 pounds, alternatively, eight 90 pound rockets together with two 250 pound bombs.

Bristol Blenheim

In 1935 the prototype Blenheim proved faster than any fighter. By 1939 it was outclassed by most German types but, although swiftly withdrawn from bombing operations, it served on as a radar-equipped night-fighter, and later as an advanced crew trainer.

Driven by two 905 horsepower Bristol Mercury Fifteen radial engines, a representative Blenheim had a ceiling of 27,000 feet, a cruising speed of 198 mph (172 knots) and a range of 1,460 miles.

Armed with two 0.303 inch (7.7 mm) calibre machine guns in a power-operated dorsal turret, with two remotely-controlled guns below the nose, and a fifth in the port wing, it could also carry a 1,300 pound load of bombs.

De Havilland Mosquito

The private-venture de Havilland Mosquito, conceived in 1938 as a fast, high-flying bomber, first flew in November 1940. The wooden construction saved on scarce alloys, the 1,620 horsepower Rolls-Royce Merlin 25 in-line engines giving a cruising speed of 325 mph (283 knots) and a ceiling of 33,000 feet, the range being 1,650 miles.

Crewed by a pilot and navigator sitting side-by-side, the aircraft flew in many roles: photo-reconnaissance (often unarmed), bomber, intruder, fighter-bomber, night-fighter, and communications-cum-freighter. There were several variants and the Mosquito remained in RAF service until 1961.

Armed versions typically carried four, 20 mm (0.79 inch) calibre cannon and four 0.303 inch (7.7 mm) calibre machine guns in the nose, together with 2,000 pounds of bombs.

De Havilland DH82A Tiger Moth

The RAF version of the tandem, two-seater biplane de Havilland Moth came into service in late 1934 and was used at over eighty wartime elementary flying training schools.

A 130 horsepower de Havilland Gipsy Major in-line engine gave it a cruising speed of 93 mph (80 knots), a ceiling of 13,000 feet and a range of 300 miles. To maintain the centre of gravity, a solo pilot sat in the rear seat. Although demanding to fly accurately, and invariably giving a freezing-cold ride, the Tiger Moth had no vices.

Douglas A-20, Havoc, or Boston

The American A-20 was variously employed as medium bomber, fighter-bomber, night-fighter and night intruder. The crew comprised pilot, navigator and gunner.

In an early night-fighter conversion, the bomb-aimer's glazed station was replaced by an opaque nose carrying eight machine guns. The RAF called this modified variant, the Havoc. However, when the Americans began their own operations in July 1942 and called their A-20G ground-attack variant the Havoc, the RAF, to avoid confusion, termed their own A-20s Bostons.

Twin 1,600 horsepower Wright Cyclone engines gave a typical A-20 a top speed of over 304 mph (264 knots), a cruise of 250 mph (217 knots), and a ceiling of 24,250 feet. The range was 1,020 miles with the maximum bomb load.

Armament varied widely depending upon the variant, but a typical fit was four fixed 0.303 inch (7.7 mm) calibre machine guns in the nose with another two pairs in the dorsal and ventral positions. There was also provision for carrying two 1,000 pound bombs. The type was noteworthy as the first operational aircraft in RAF service to have a tricycle undercarriage.

Douglas Dakota (DC-3)

The 1935 Douglas DC-3, Dakota, the doyen of air transports, was still flying commercially in 2010. Initially it carried a crew of three and twenty-one passengers but its roles have been manifold.

Typical performance figures based upon two 1,000 horsepower Wright Cyclone radial engines, are a maximum speed of 220 mph (191 knots), a cruising speed of 194 mph (169 knots), a stalling speed of 67 mph (58 knots), and a ceiling of 21,900 feet. The range is 2,125 miles.

Fairey Battle

The 1936 single-engined Fairey Battle light bomber was obsolete when war broke out. Accommodating a pilot, bomb-aimer/observer and a wireless operator/air gunner, the Battle, powered by a 1,030 horsepower Rolls-Royce

Merlin Mk.1 in-line engine, cruised at 210 mph (182 knots) at up to 25,000 feet and had a range of 1,000 miles. It had a bomb load of 1,000 pounds.

For defence it had a Vickers 0.303 inch (7.7 mm) calibre machine gun in a rear-cockpit mounting, and another in the starboard wing. Being totally outclassed by German fighters it was swiftly withdrawn as a day bomber, continuing to serve, however, in the training and target-towing roles.

Handley Page Halifax

The seven-crewed, twin-finned Halifax heavy bomber entered RAF service in November 1940. The type was also employed in the transport and maritime roles, and as an ambulance and glider tug. It was also widely used for

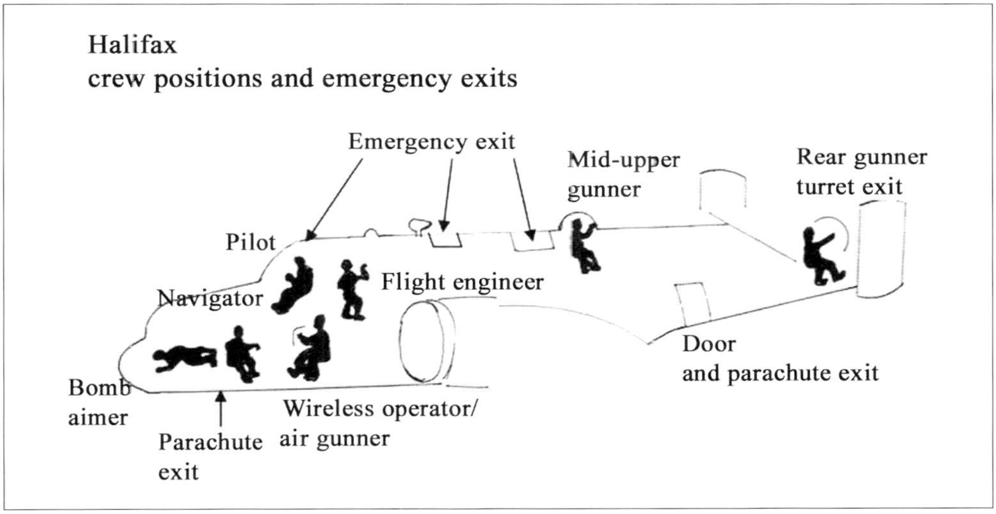

paratrooping and supply dropping, often in clandestine settings.

A typical fit of four 1,615 horsepower Bristol Hercules Sixteen radial engines gave a cruising speed of 215 mph (187 knots) and a ceiling of 24,000 feet. The Halifax's range was 1,030 miles, and it could carry 13,000 pounds of bombs. As defensive armament it had nine 0.303 inch (7.7 mm) calibre machine guns; one in the nose, and four each in dorsal and tail turrets. After some early stalling accidents the leading-edge profile of the tailfins was altered from pointed to square: the photo illustrates the early shape, the diagram the modified one.

Handley Page Hampden

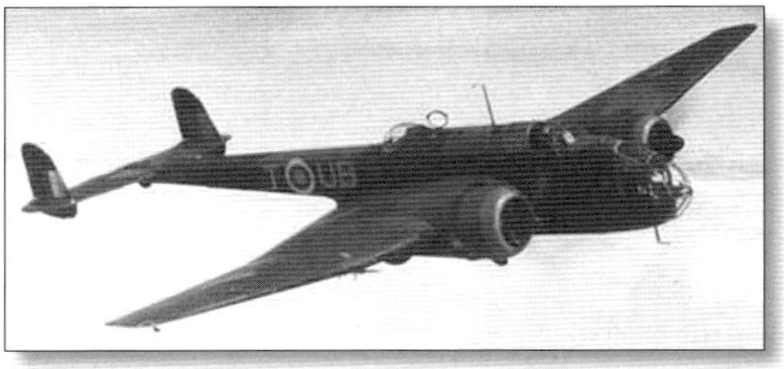

The 1936 four-crewed Hampden was powered by two 1,000 horsepower, 9-cylinder, Bristol Pegasus Mark Eighteen radial engines. Contemporary performance figures vary from the manufacturer's 'incredibly fast' 254 mph (221 knots) maximum speed, through 217 mph (189 knots), with actual users reporting 130 mph (113 knots). The least sanguine modern source proffers 167 mph (145 knots). The ceiling, likewise, is frequently given as 19,000 feet although the manufacturers only claimed 15,000 feet.

Irreconcilable figures aside, the Hampden's Handley Page leading-edge slots gave it a landing speed of just 73 mph (64 knots). Further, it had a range of 1,200 miles with a full bomb load of 4,000 pounds, extending to 1,885 miles carrying just 2,000 pounds. Defensive armament was two, forward-firing 0.303 inch (7.7 mm) calibre machine guns, with additional twin mountings in both a dorsal and a rearward-facing belly position.

The Hampden was swiftly removed from bomber operations and employed in torpedo dropping, minelaying, night operations and leaflet dropping. It was regarded as pleasant to handle, although the crew, isolated from one another though they were, found their positions cramped.

North American Harvard

After its 1935 debut, over 17,000 Harvard advanced trainers were built. Used by the RAF from January 1939, it remained in service until 1955.

The typical engine fit was a 550/600 horsepower, 9-cylinder Pratt and Whitney Wasp engine, air-cooled and driving a Hamilton two-bladed, two-position controllable-pitch propeller. The top speed was 206 mph (179 knots) the cruise 180 mph (156 knots) and the landing speed 63 mph (55 knots). The ceiling was 23,000 feet and the range 730 miles.

Although popular, the Harvard was a demanding machine, and therefore, a good advanced trainer. Delivered early to the French government, a hundred Harvards were used by the Luftwaffe for training and for familiarising those pilots required to evaluate captured American machines. The South African Air Force retained the type until 1995.

North American P-51 Mustang

Only after December 1943, when Rolls-Royce Merlin-engined, long-range-escort Mustangs arrived in Europe, could the hard-pressed American bomber crews be given fighter support throughout an entire mission.

Typical performance figures based upon the 1,520 horsepower Packard Rolls-Royce Merlin V-1650-3 liquid-cooled engine driving a Curtiss electric constant-speed propeller, give a maximum speed of 425 mph (369 knots) and a ceiling of over 40,000 feet. The Mustang's range was in excess of a thousand miles.

Armament carried was six or eight 0.5 inch (12.7 mm) calibre machine guns, or four 20 mm (0.79 inch) calibre cannon, with 1,000 pounds of bombs mounted underwing.

Short Stirling

The Short Stirling was the first of the RAF's heavy bombers. Shorts reused their successful Sunderland-wing profile but Ministry requirements limited the span to 100 feet (not, as widely stated,

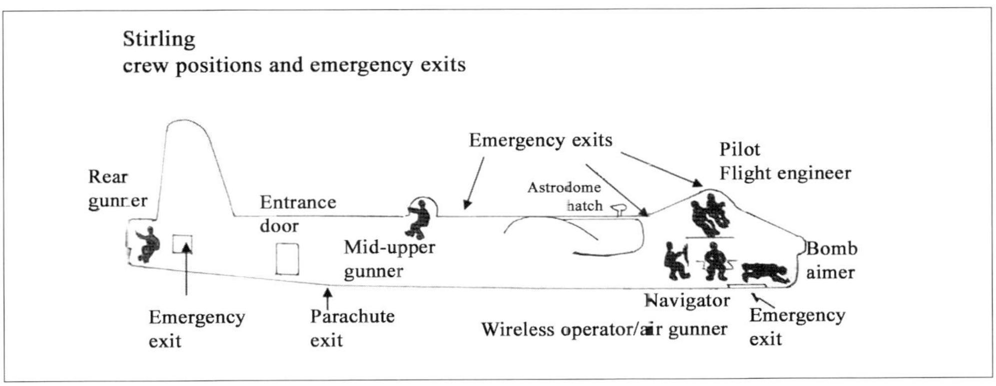

to fit into RAF hangars, which were 125 feet wide). This, and similar modifications, detracted from the design performance to give the Stirling a ceiling of only 17,000 feet.

It was, however, very manoeuvrable, and powered by four 1,650 horsepower Bristol Hercules Sixteen radial engines, had a maximum speed of 270 mph (235 knots), a cruise of 200 mph (174 knots) and a range – dependent upon bomb load – of up to 2,000 miles.

The Stirling carried 14,000 pounds of bombs, and had eight 0.303 inch (7.7 mm) calibre machine guns; four in a tail turret, and two each in nose and dorsal turrets. Its cockpit stood at a lofty 22 feet 9 inches above the tarmac.

It was popular with its seven- or eight-man crews but its bomb bay could not be adapted to the bigger ordnance being developed and it ceased bomber operations in September 1941. It was then very successfully employed in the glider-tug, transport, and clandestine-operations roles; 1,759 bombers were produced, also 160 transport variants.

Supermarine Spitfire

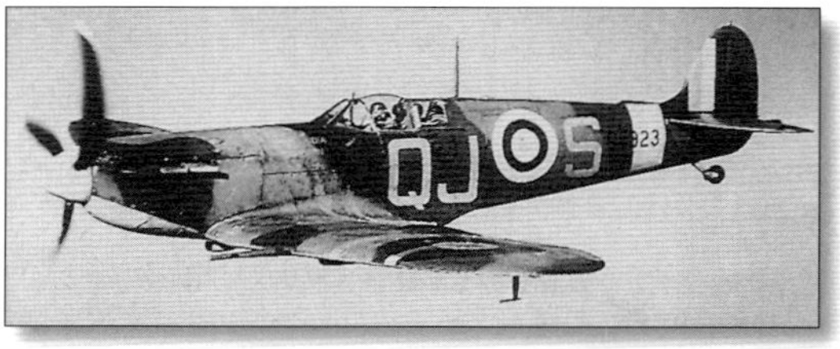

The Spitfire first flew in March 1936 and metamorphosed through over a score of variant Marks which befitted it to all single-engined tasks. Production finished in October 1947, 23,000 Spitfires having been built.

Representative performance figures for early versions with the 1,030 horsepower Rolls-Royce Merlin Mark Two in-line engine, driving a two-bladed, wooden, fixed-pitch propeller, gave a maximum speed of 350 mph (304 knots), a cruising speed of 265 mph (230 knots) and a ceiling of 30,500 feet. Range was 630 miles. Armament was eight, 0.303 inch (7.7 mm) calibre wing-mounted machine guns.

Later performance figures, based upon the 2,035 horsepower, supercharged Griffon engine, give a maximum speed of 448 mph (389 knots), time to 20,000 feet of seven minutes, and range, with external tank, of 850 miles. A regular armament fit became two 20 mm (0.79 inch) cannon and four 0.303 inch (7.7 mm) calibre machine guns; although the latter were eventually replaced by two 0.5 inch (12.7 mm) calibre machine guns.

Vickers Wellington

In designing the 1937-vintage five- or six-crewed Wellington, the celebrated Barnes Wallis used repeated junctions of Meccano-like alloy channels to form a cocoon of great strength. This geodetic (see glossary) structure was then covered with doped fabric.

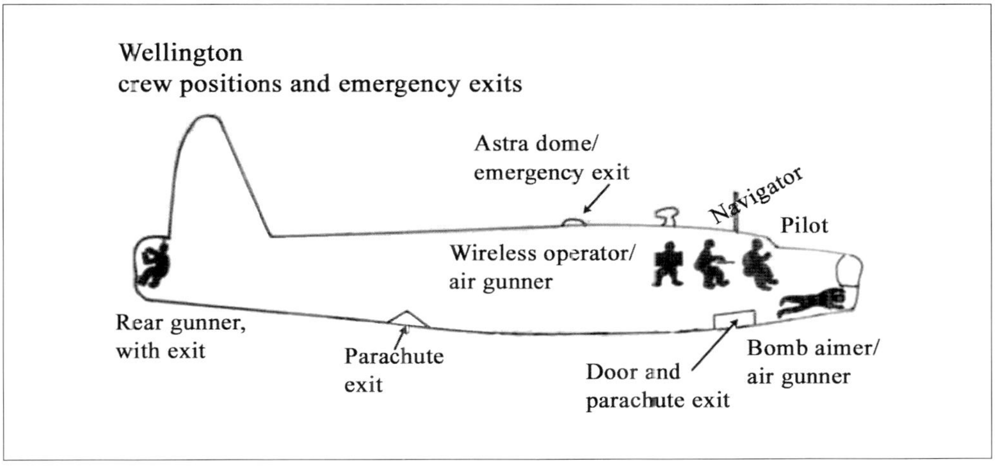

The German defences soon took the Wellington's measure, after which it was switched to night bombing. However, Wellingtons were also employed in the maritime role, using metal coils to detonate magnetic mines and locating submarines with the aid of Air-to-Surface-Vessel radar (ASV) and Leigh searchlights. The Wellington ceased service in 1953.

A typical power fit was two 1,500 horsepower Bristol Hercules Eleven radial engines which gave a ceiling of 19,000 feet and a maximum speed of 235 mph (204 knots). Representative cruising speeds vary with source, ranging from 232 mph (202 knots) to 166 mph (144 knots). A former Wellington pilot suggested 173 mph (150 knots), with a normal bombing altitude of 12,000 feet.

The bomb load was 4,500 pounds and the armament eight 0.303 inch (7.7 mm) calibre machine guns; four in the tail turret, two in the beam, and two in the nose.

Enemy machines

Messerschmitt Bf109

The 1935-designed Messerschmitt Bf109 was modified throughout the war but was typically powered by a 1,475 Daimler-Benz twelve-cylinder, liquid-cooled engine which gave it a maximum speed of 386 mph (335 knots) at 22,640 feet and an initial rate of climb of 3,346 feet a minute. It had a range of 620 miles and commonly carried two 7.9 mm (0.31 inch) machine guns and a 20 mm (0.79 inch) cannon; later, a 30 mm (1.18 inch) cannon.

Trials found the Spitfire and the Bf109 to be evenly matched between 12,000 and 17,000 feet with the Bf109 performing better above 20,000 feet. 35,000 were built.

Messerschmitt Bf110

The 'Destroyer' variant of the twin-engined, twin-crewed Messerschmitt Bf110 – a type designed in 1936 – was powered by two Daimler-Benz 1,475 horsepower engines which gave a maximum speed of 352 mph (306 knots), a ceiling of 26,000 feet, time to 20,000 feet of nine minutes, and a range of 745 miles. Later variants would carry a third crew member.

Typical armament was two nose-mounted 20 mm (0.79 inch) cannon and four 7.9 mm (0.31 inch) machine guns, plus another in the rear cockpit. There was also provision for two more forward-firing 20 mm cannon in an underbelly tray. The night-fighter variant carried a 30 mm (1.18 inch) cannon and others had the twin *Scräge Musik* upward-firing 30 mm cannon.

Junkers Ju88

The Junkers Ju88 bomber, conceived in 1936, was eminently successful in many roles, a typical engine fit of two 1,400 horsepower Junkers 211J liquid-cooled inverted V12 engines giving it a maximum speed of 295 mph (256 knots) and a ceiling of 26,900 feet. The four-crew variant carried a pilot, a bomb aimer, a top-gunner/radio-operator, and a lower-gunner/flight-engineer.

Representative armament was three forward-firing 7.9 mm (0.31 inch) calibre machine guns and a 20 mm (0.79 inch) cannon, together with two 7.9 mm machine guns in the dorsal and ventral turrets. It carried four 550 kilogram bombs.

Focke-Wulf FW190

The 1941 Focke-Wulf FW190 evolved through forty variants but typically its maximum speed was 408 mph (355 knots) with a time to 29,000 feet of twenty minutes, a ceiling of 37,000 feet, a range of 500 miles, and a combat endurance of one hour.

Many carried four 7.92 mm (0.31 inch) machine guns and two 20 mm (0.79 inch) cannon; later versions employed 30 mm (1.18 inch) cannon. Additionally the FW190 could carry a wide range of underslung rockets.

A comparison flight with a relatively early mark of Spitfire showed the FW190 to be superior in all respects except for turning capability.

Messerschmitt Me262

Appearing in 1944, the single-seater Messerschmitt Me262 interceptor-fighter was the first jet into operational service, its two 1,980 pound static-thrust Jumo turbojet engines giving it a maximum speed of 540 mph (469 knots) and an initial rate of climb of 4,000 feet a minute. The night-fighter version was equipped with intercept radar as well as a device for homing onto British H2S-radar transmissions.

Typical armament was four 30 mm (1.18 inch) cannon, together with twenty-four 55 mm (2.2 inch) rockets in underwing racks.

Messerschmitt Me163 Komet

A Walter two-rocket motor giving 3,750 pounds of thrust for 7.5 minutes gave the swept-wing target-defence Messerschmitt Me163 a maximum speed of 593 mph (518 knots), a initial rate of climb of 15,950 feet a minute, a ceiling of 40,000 feet and a radius of action of 22 miles.

Armament was two wing-rooted 30 mm (1.18 inch) cannon. Among many problems experienced by the type the difficulties of high-speed handling extended to those of aiming at slower-flying bombers.

V1 (*Vergeltungswaffe*) Flying Bomb

The German *Fern Ziel Geraet* (effectively: Long-range Aiming Apparatus), their *Vergeltungswaffe 1* (Reprisal Weapon Number One), was a pilotless flying bomb. It

might be politic to emphasise that the V1 – nowadays too-often termed 'V1 *rocket*' – was a pulse-jet aircraft.

The first test flight was in December 1941, the main assault on Britain and Belgium beginning in June 1944 and lasting eighty days. It is held that of 10,000 V1s launched against England, 7,000 landed on the mainland.

The V1 was propelled up a railed launching ramp by volatile hydrogen peroxide, and then accelerated to 410 mph (356 knots) by an Argus AS14 pulse-jet which developed 660 pounds of static thrust. The V1 was given a range of 150 miles by 750 gallons of petrol, the total weight of 4,750 pounds including nearly a ton of amatol high-explosive. While normally ramp-launched, 825 V1s were carried beneath Heinkel One-Eleven bombers.

In flight, an auto-pilot would hold the heading and height, while a propeller-driven timer would decide the range. At the pre-determined time, a linkage would set the elevator to dive. The abrupt nose-down impetus had the effect of cutting the engine, so leading to the cessation of sound which warned the initiated that an explosion was imminent.

Enemy defences

Anti-aircraft guns

The main German anti-aircraft weapon was the 88 mm (3.5 inch) calibre cannon which, even in the early years, could effectively fire fifteen high-explosive shells a minute to a height of 26,000 feet: 2,000 feet above the average bomber's ceiling. Yet development soon allowed the 88s to reach an effective 37,000 feet at a firing rate of twenty rounds a minute. Besides that, the shells themselves changed their nature, first showering out shrapnel, then in spraying incendiary pellets beyond the shrapnel burst.

15,000 flak guns formed successive ten-mile-wide defensive belts across Holland and Germany, the guns being integrated with a control system whose master searchlight would lead up to sixteen others to cone any bomber targeted.

In Germany's major centres, the heavier calibre 128 mm (5 inch) guns, capable of firing ten rounds a minute to 35,000 feet, were sited in permanent flak towers.

A flak tower.

Glossary

Aircrew Europe Star: a well-thought-of award for air operations carried out over Europe from Britain between 3 September 1939 and 5 June 1944.

Arriving, Arrival chit: when reporting on posting 'Arriving' personnel would check in, on signature, at every section on the station relevant to them (clothing stores, accounts) so that they were known to be on strength for issues and services. Similarly, personnel would 'Clear' with their 'clearance chits', on being posted away.

ATS: Auxiliary Territorial Service: the women's army, WRAC (Women's Royal Army Corps) from 1949.

AI: Airborne Interception radar. The ground controller would direct the aircraft to a target. The airborne operator would then use his radar display to home the pilot to within visual range of the target.

Aircrew: on 19 January 1939 non-commissioned aircrew (gunners) were effectively afforded the status of sergeants, although the situation was not regularised until early 1940 when heavy bombers appeared. World War Two categories comprised: pilot; navigator (observer, pre-1942); wireless operator/air gunner; air gunner; flight engineer (post 1941); bomb aimer (post 1942). This omits the navigator/wireless operator category, and several similar combinations involving navigators.

ASV: Air Surface Vessel. A map-presentation radar, similar to H2S, designed for maritime use.

Bombs: in general, these only become armed after a time-delay. On the smaller bombs, a spin vane would set this delay; on larger ones an additional spin vane would arm the bomb to explode on impact after that delay.

Bullseye: a sortie designed to simulate an operation. It might involve photographing a UK target or approaching an enemy coast as a diversion.

Caterpillar Club: after Lieutenant Harold R Hams escaped by parachute from his disabled aircraft in America on 20 October 1922, a club was formed for those who were forced to make an emergency descent. The Caterpillar symbol was chosen because early parachutes were made of silk, and the insect had to leave its cocoon in order to fly.

Commissioned officer: one appointed by the sovereign. A warrant officer is a very senior non-commissioned officer appointed by the Service authority.

Cookie: a finless, thin-cased, 4,000 pound bomb.

Cook's tour: flights laid on after VE Day, often to show non-aircrew personnel the former target areas.

Corkscrew: an evasion manoeuvre in which the aircraft was dived steeply and hastily, then climbed, banking – 'winging over' – throughout.

Darky: a get-you-home service which utilised the short range of airborne VHF (voice) sets. Actually hearing an aircraft call meant that it was close. The Darky station could, therefore, use its own location to pass the aircraft a heading to a suitable airfield. Other Darky stations on the way to that airfield, alerted of the aircraft's approach by telephone, would refine the heading.

D-Day: 6 June 1944. The invasion of Europe, launched in the Cherbourg-Peninsular area.

Dicey: dangerous.

'E' Boats: *Schnellboot* or S-boot (fast craft), German torpedo boats.

EFTS: Elementary Flying Training School. Basic flying was taught but the unit could also be used as a Grading School, where aspirant pilots were allowed fifteen hours' flying during which their suitability for further training would be assessed.

Elsan: a chemical toilet, often situated near the tail, therefore a visit made at altitude meant using the emergency oxygen bottle and going off intercom.

Empire, or Commonwealth, Air Training Scheme: set up in 1939 to take advantage of the favourable flying conditions in various Commonwealth countries. Discontinued in late 1944.

Feather: to electrically or hydraulically turn the blades of a stopped propeller edge-on to the airflow to cut down the drag, as with an oar in rowing. The propeller of a failed engine left blade-on to the airflow, and therefore, said to be 'windmilling', creates an inordinate amount of drag.

FIDO: Fog, Investigation and Dispersal Operation. A landing aid in which burning petrol was used to locally heat the air along the runway to, effectively, temporarily disperse the fog. It took twenty minutes to become effective. From 1943 FIDO was installed at fifteen British airfields and was credited with allowing 2,500 aircraft to recover.

Flak: enemy anti-aircraft gunfire, from *flugabwehrkanone* (aircraft defence cannon). The Allied equivalent was Ack Ack, using the pre-1924 phonetic for AA, anti-aircraft. The 'modern' term anti-aircraft-artillery (AAA) was, in fact, contemporary to the period, though rarely used.

'G' Force: apparent increase in body weight when turning tightly or pulling out of a manoeuvre.

Gazette (gazetted): *The London Gazette* ('Published by Authority') promulgates awards.

Gee (box): Ground Electronic Equipment. A radar aid by which master and slave ground-station signals were plotted on a lattice chart to give a very accurate fix. Gee's range was 350 to 400 miles.

Gen: reliable information. Duff gen, false information.

Geodetic: the structure developed by Sir Barnes Wallis and employed in the Wellington bomber. Essentially, it comprised triangular grids made up of aluminium strips to form a mutually-supporting shell of great strength. More properly, the component parts formed 'geodetic' curves (parts of a circle) on the structure, each element taking the shortest line across the curved surface.

Good conduct stripe: an inverted chevron worn low on the left sleeve.

Goolie chit: a multi-language statement which promises a reward to those who aid downed airmen: apparently (SOED) from Hindustani for ball.

Green endorsement: a complimentary entry made in an aircrew member's flying log book.

Gremlins: manikins whose *raison d'être* was to harass aircrew by creating technical problems. They appeared in 1940, got into print in the *RAF Journal* in 1942, indoctrinated fighter pilot Roald Dahl a little later and subsequently Walt Disney. Known to be 'green, gamboge and gold; male, female and neuter; and both young and old', yet there were fliers who thought them fictitious.

H2S: map-presentation radar. Originally, BN: Blind Navigation. Until a scientist observed, 'the whole thing is stinking through not having been done years ago.' Hence, H2S, the hydrogen sulphide smell of bad eggs.

'You have control', 'I have control': procedural formula used to ensure that there is no doubt which of two pilots is controlling the aircraft.

ITW: Initial Training Wing. The training unit which taught drill and elementary air-related subjects.

Kriegie: *kriegsgefangener*, prisoner of war.

LMF: Lack of Moral Fibre. The term the RAF used during the Second World War for combat fatigue or post-traumatic stress disorder. Since the 1700s also known as Nostalgia, Melancholia, Hysteria, Wavering, Shellshock, and Flying Sickness D (debility).

Mention (in Despatches): recognition of a job well done, but not meriting actual decoration or award.

Milk-run: an easy sortie.

Missions: see Operations, ops.

Monica: a rearward-looking radar for detecting attacking fighters whose use was discontinued because German fighters could home onto it.

'My weapon is bent': code for 'my radar is unserviceable'.

Nickel: a propaganda-leaflet drop.

Oboe: a blind bombing aid employing two ground stations. Essentially, one provided a beam to lead the aircraft over the target, the other told it the bomb-release point. With stations at Dover and Cromer, it was first used against a Ruhr target on 21 December 1942, with an accuracy of some 80 yards. After the invasion 24 mobile stations were placed on the continent.

Operations, Ops: throughout the Second World War, offensive sorties by the RAF against the enemy were termed operational flights, or ops. The equivalent term employed by the United States Army Air Force was missions. While there were variations in the

rules by which RAF operations were reckoned, even within Bomber Command, the standard operational tour required may be taken as thirty.
OTU: Operational Training Unit. The unit at which aircrew were made familiar with the machines and the techniques of the Commands they were to join.
Port/starboard: viewed looking forwards.
Psycho device: this encoded plain language for transmission by morse code.
RAAF: Royal Australian Air Force.
RCAF: Royal Canadian Air Force.
RNZAF: Royal New Zealand Air Force.
S-boat: *Schnellboot*, fast, small vessel.
Stooge about: to fly without purpose, or to patrol an area while alert for opportunity targets.
Supercharger gears: a supercharger compresses the rarefied air at altitude back to sea-level pressure. During the era considered, at about 12,000 feet, as the manifold pressure began to fall despite the throttle being fully open, the pilot would ease back the throttle, select the higher gear, then advance the throttle to get the required manifold pressure.
Tallboy L(arge): 22,000 pound bomb, designed for deep penetration; Grand Slam.
Tallboy M(edium): 12,000 pound medium-capacity bomb.
U-boat: *Unterseeboot*, submarine.
***Vertuti Militari*:** Polish decoration (pronounced Ver-tooty Meellee-tar-ee).
V1: *Vergeltungswaffe 1* (Reprisal Weapon) unmanned Fiesler 103 pulse-jet flying bomb.
V2: *Vergeltungswaffe 2* (Reprisal Weapon) A-4 ground to ground rocket.
V3: *Vergeltungswaffe 3* (Reprisal Weapon) rocket-boosted, long-range gun.
VE Day: 8 May 1945. Victory in Europe, end of war in Europe.
VHF: very high frequency.
VJ Day: 15 August 1945 in UK. Victory over Japan, end of Second World War.
Windmilling: see Feather.
Window: strips of paper-backed aluminium foil, sized in relation to the wavelength of the enemy radar, and air-dropped to interfere with its displays.
Woodbridge (Suffolk): along with Manston (Kent), and Carnaby (Yorkshire), emergency airfields, 3,000 yards long, 250 yards wide, in three strips with extensive grassed under- and over-shoot areas.

Selective References

Air Ministry (1937), *Royal Air Force Pocket Book, AP1081*. London: HMSO

Air Ministry (1943), *Elementary Flying Training, AP1979A.* London: HMSO

Air Ministry (1948), *The Rise and Fall of the German Air Force (1931 to 1945).* London: HMSO

Air Ministry (1954), *Flying, Volumes 1 and 2, AP129.* (Sixth edition). London: HMSO

Bennett, D.C.T. (1936), *The Complete Air Navigator.* London: Pitman

Fellowes, P. F. M. (1942), *Britain's Wonderful Air Force.* London: Odhams

Handley Page Ltd (1949), *Forty Years On*. London: Handley Page

HMSO (1944), *Target: Germany*. London: Air Ministry

Monday, David (1982), *British Aircraft of World War II*. Chancellor Press: London

Stewart, Oliver. (1941), *The Royal Air Force in Pictures.* London: Country Life

Thetford, Owen (1958), *Aircraft of the Royal Air Force 1918-58.* London: Putnam

Other books by the author:

Non-fiction

High Peak Air Crash Sites, Central Area (Countryside Books) ISBN 978 1 84674 219 4

Peakland Aircrashes Series: *The South* (2005); *The Central Area* (2006); *The North* (2006

Blind Faith: Joan Waste, Derby's Martyr ISBN 978 0 9556325 1 8

Fiction

A Magnificent Diversion: series (Acclaimed by the First World War Aviation Historical Society's *Cross and Cockade International*)

The Infinite Reaches 1915-16, ISBN 978 0 9556325 25

Contact Patrol 1916, ISBN 978 0 9556325 3 2

Sold A Pup 1917, ISBN 978 0 9556325 4 9

The Great Disservice 1918, ISBN 978 0 9556325 5 6

In Kinder's Mists (a Kinder ghost story) ISBN 978 0 9556325 0 1

'Though the Treason Pleases' (Irish Troubles) ISBN 978 0 9556325 6 3